ADVERTISING
TRANSFORMED

❖ IN PRAISE OF ❖
ADVERTISING TRANSFORMED

'At last a thorough study on the role and value of advertising today. Fons van Dyck analyzes, synthesizes and presents the advertising professionals a mirror for the future, in a way only he can.' **Jan-Willem Vosmeer, Manager CSR, Heineken International**

'In today's fragmented environment, building brand awareness is more important than ever to win a share of the hearts and wallets of fickle consumers. Communication guru Fons van Dyck cracks the codes of effective ad campaigns, combining conventional wisdom, new research insights and current best-practice illustrations.' **Joeri Van den Bergh, author, *How Cool Brands Stay Hot*, Founder, InSites Consulting**

'A strong combination of scientific research and real-life case studies. Fons van Dyck effortlessly combines these two worlds and adds his vast experience to provide compelling insights. A refreshing book for every communications professional.' **Nils van Dam, Country Manager, Unilever Belgium and Luxembourg**

'Advertising still works in these digital times. Yet, advertising has to adapt to new technologies and new consumer habits. Fons van Dyck guides us in an accessible way on a well-documented journey through the world of advertising in the 21st century. A must-read for everyone in the marketing industry.' **Steven Van Belleghem, author, *The Conversation Manager***

ADVERTISING
TRANSFORMED

THE NEW RULES FOR THE DIGITAL AGE

FONS VAN DYCK

KoganPage

Publisher's note

Every possible effort has been made to ensure that the information contained in this book is accurate at the time of going to press, and the publishers and author cannot accept responsibility for any errors or omissions, however caused. No responsibility for loss or damage occasioned to any person acting, or refraining from action, as a result of the material in this publication can be accepted by the editor, the publisher or the author.

First published in Great Britain and the United States in 2014 by Kogan Page Limited

2nd Floor, 45 Gee Street
London EC1V 3RS
United Kingdom
www.koganpage.com

1518 Walnut Street, Suite 1100
Philadelphia PA 19102
USA

4737/23 Ansari Road
Daryaganj
New Delhi 110002
India

© Fons Van Dyck, 2014

The right of Fons Van Dyck to be identified as the author of this work has been asserted by him in accordance with the Copyright, Designs and Patents Act 1988.

ISBN   978 0 7494 7148 4
E-ISBN   978 0 7494 7149 1

British Library Cataloguing-in-Publication Data

A CIP record for this book is available from the British Library.

Library of Congress Cataloging-in-Publication Data

Van Dyck, Fons.
   Advertising transformed : the new rules for the digital age / Fons Van Dyck.
      pages cm
   Includes bibliographical references.
   ISBN 978-0-7494-7148-4 – ISBN 978-0-7494-7149-1 (ebk)   1. Advertising.   2. Advertising–
Technological innovations.   3. Internet advertising.   4. Digital media.   I. Title.
   HF5823.V24 2014
   659.1–dc23

                                                                              2013044127

Typeset by Graphicraft Limited, Hong Kong
Print production managed by Jellyfish
Printed and bound by CPI Group (UK) Ltd, Croydon CR0 4YY

✦ CONTENTS ✦

✤ LIST OF FIGURES ✤

❖ LIST OF TABLES ❖

✤ FOREWORD ✤ BY LUC SUYKENS

There's no crisis, there's only a new reality

As markets mature, first they segment, then they fragment. Many European and US consumer goods companies have, over the past few years, launched flankers and line extensions targeting increasingly more niche markets. Marketers hoped thereby to earn more money from current customers by trading them up to premium products. Overall, the majority of marketing budgets were going to increasingly smaller flankers and line extensions.

As a consequence of this shift in budgets, the core of the brand has been getting less attention and support. The proposition of the brand is getting less clear to consumers. As A-brands are less able to differentiate themselves from Private Labels, these cheaper imitations are growing faster. Brands are losing the trust of consumers, while trust is exactly what brands are supposed to offer. This is especially true in times of crisis, when consumers seek to avoid risk and are in search of proven values; brands should be flourishing instead of suffering.

To regain trust, we are looking to broaden the definition of the 'brand'. First of all the basic values of the brand need to be restored and regain the central position in the advertising. However, that won't be enough. Today's critical consumer asks more questions and looks for information on the company behind the brand. This is not completely new, as we have always been used to knowing 'someone who knows someone' who is working at the local brewery, and understands how things work within a certain national company. This informal connection that once existed between a company and its customer has decreased in a 'globalizing' world. Such a distance demands that companies – especially global ones – actively communicate about their values that were once controlled implicitly. Of course, one can only communicate about values when the company actually behaves in accordance with them. As is the case with friendships, trust builds up slowly, but can be lost overnight.

The idea behind the brand shall therefore be defined broader than ever before. In today's literature, it is often referred to as the 'purpose' or 'brand ideal'. It is born from 'the category experience', but clearly differentiating the brand in that experience. For instance, the Apple brand experience is not only to provide a well-operating and smoothly designed computer; the brand also reflects the value of inspiration: 'Think different'. Pampers, as a second example, offers a functional and dry diaper, but the brand's appeal goes beyond that. It wants to support 'baby development'. This brand ideal or purpose drives the complete brand experience, especially the innovation and advertising strategy.

A well-defined idea allows for consistency over time. The importance of consistency has been heavily undervalued in advertising, where awards are mostly distributed for creativity. Real creativity, however, requires innovation that is in line with a consistent brand purpose and its past. This is exactly why Fons Van Dyck's book points out the Effie awards that celebrate effectiveness of campaigns over a longer period of time and reward brand consistency. The essence of advertising is to use the idea to generate trial and to find new users to discover and use the brand. In marketing the Mattëus principle is at play as well: 'the rich get richer and the poor get poorer'. Brands with more users will gain in loyalty and repurchase numbers. The bigger brands will only get bigger and will be the ones to catch the majority of profit within the category.

The book also shows how light users must be attracted in order to maintain a large user base. Pampers is an extreme example in this regard as they renew their user group every two years. Every year, a brand must be fed with a new load of users and that is exactly the core job of advertising. Users should be attracted by the idea, not the price. When price is the customer's only motivation to try out a new brand, he or she will hop straight to the competition when they launch their next promotion. Therefore, the brand idea should be consistent over time and creativity is there to keep the idea relevant and appealing.

I'm convinced that the current complexity of the media environment is a blessing for marketers. Although marketing might have been simpler before, we were never able to build such strong brands. Media consumption was mainly limited to television, radio and press. Translating your message into a 30-second television commercial or a one-page advertisement was the main challenge. Today's consumers use more media at once and spend many hours behind their computer, tablet or smartphone, which makes it less easy to reach them.

Today, marketers are in the position of being able to use many different media, each with their specific advantages, and therefore they are able to work in a more nuanced manner. All the different media together create a complete experience so that our message need no longer be squeezed only into a 30-second time frame. It is now possible to advocate the idea behind the brand in a way far richer than before. We still believe in TV commercials to communicate a brand like Pampers, as these commercials allow them to explain the 'dry bums' USP or the Unicef Alliance ESP that supports underprivileged babies. But we can make the message more profound by means of an online campaign, where Pampers helps you choose the right diaper variant, based on your baby's age. The Facebook page offers a platform for young mothers to share experiences and to ask the brand questions. Before, the mother had to send out a letter and often wait several weeks for a reply. Everything moves much faster now and most users know about the brand's possible problems. Both the user and marketer benefit from the increased transparency when the goal is to truly improve the brand. Bad intentions will be revealed faster as well, and this is not only due to the internet, but to the brand issue itself, which would have come out in the open sooner or later.

This increasing complexity in terms of media use requires a new organizational structure. The brand manager should still lead the brand: he needs to know the consumer, drive the innovation strategy and integrate advertising campaigns. In addition, we need to rely on communication experts who exploit the idea, fully leveraging the strength of their medium. When all the different media are able to enrich the message in their own way, the total message will become more powerful.

I fully believe that the new reality will allow us to create stronger brands and attract more people by means of appealing advertising. How to do this exactly is explained in detail by this book.

Luc Suykens
Harley Procter Marketing Director
Procter & Gamble

✤ FOREWORD BY ✤ STEPHAN LOERKE

Advertising Transformed gives the reader a compelling view of the new world of advertising at a time of unprecedented change. The book has a strong academic foundation, yet importantly, it features a lot of highly relevant case studies which provide solid strategic insights for marketers.

Among the key trends reshaping the world of advertising, Van Dyck identifies three in particular: the emergence of the unfaithful consumer ('the light buyer'), the complementary nature of traditional media and digital platforms and the ever more important role of creativity – which builds business and generates return on investment (ROI).

Advertising as we have known it is probably almost dead – long live advertising! It is being reinvented, and this book provides fascinating insights to those who are interested in understanding the new paradigm. Fons Van Dyck hits the nail on the head when he quotes Darwin: 'It's not the strongest species that survives, nor most intelligent. It is the one that is the most adaptable to change.'

This is an excellent read for anyone wishing to understand the future of advertising.

Stephan Loerke
Managing Director
World Federation of Advertisers (WFA)

✤ PREFACE ✤

Early in 1998, the Belgian telco start-up Telenet (today, part of Liberty Global Plc) raised its yellow tents on market squares in many Flemish cities and towns to attract its first customers in a liberalized market. As Director of Communication of the new telco brand, I saw young families with children gathering in front of a little computer screen to explore the possibilities of fast broadband Internet. For many of them, it opened up a whole new world.

In those days, Telenet's marketing was a matter of going from one town to another. Some called it 'nomad marketing', and it was based on an unprecedented local marketing strategy. Local stakeholders were included in the approach: from mayors and local aldermen to the presidents of cultural associations. The impact was huge. In every local community and in no time at all, Telenet was – literally and figuratively – the talk of the town.

Sixteen years later, the Internet has brought about a dramatic change in the way we communicate. As was the case with television in the 1960s, the Internet has produced a social and cultural revolution. Social undercurrents such as empowerment, togetherness and a fair bit of anti-establishment feeling are enabling consumers to seize power on an increasing scale. The world of marketing and advertising has changed forever.

During the last few years, I have had the chance to speak for and with marketers on many occasions. They have a lot of questions about all these changes. Old marketing recipes no longer seem to work, yet at the same time it is not exactly clear which alternatives will yield better results in the future. Not wanting to build their strategy on quicksand, they need strong foundations that go beyond the hype of the day.

The key questions I wish to address in this book are: *what is the role of advertising in brand marketing today and what is the impact of advertising on consumers in the digital age?* Or put more simply: what works best and what doesn't work?

It is a book about the real and presumed power or the lack of power that advertising has in the 21st century. It is not a scientific book, yet it is based on a personal selection of relevant scientific research. In this respect, it wants to address an existing need amongst marketing and communication professionals, by disclosing recent and relevant scientific research that can bring their theoretical knowledge up to speed.

Advertising Transformed is aimed at three specific groups of readers:

✤ Marketing and advertising professionals (advertisers, agencies, media), who are looking for theoretical insights and answers to questions from their daily practice;

✤ CEOs and general managers in companies and their procurement departments, who wish to optimize their investments in marketing and advertising;

✤ Students and lecturers in marketing and communication, offering them an overview of recent literature, tested out in practical cases.

The book is divided into three major parts:

✤ The first part indicates and discusses a number of basic insights into the way advertising works in marketing and communications planning today. What is the core target group of advertising? Which strategy works best? Do social media mean the end of advertising? Why is the integration of marketing and communication becoming increasingly important? Are consumers better at advertising?

✤ The second part addresses some of the hotter topics in current advertising practice. What works best: a USP (unique selling proposition) or an ESP (emotional selling proposition)? Is the future of advertising global or local? Is 'green' really a sales argument and, if it is, for what type of customer? What is the power of 'retro' in advertising?

✤ The third part explores the scientific evidence available today, which demonstrates the added value of marketing and advertising for companies and organizations, even in times of economic recession. In the last part, the book focuses on some of the important topics of criticism that are currently being levelled at brands and advertising in particular, and examines how brands are responding.

In conclusion, *Advertising Transformed* is not about how advertising works in the brain or the memory of consumers, nor is it about media planning. The book aims to provide strategic answers to questions from managers and marketers about the effectiveness of advertising.

Advertising Transformed does not have all the answers to these questions, nor does it pretend to be exhaustive. Instead, it seeks to provide a basis for further debate and reflection. Consequently, I would be delighted to receive your own experiences or questions via **www.advertisingtransformed.com**. This website also offers readers additional cases and updates. Please feel free to make suggestions for an 11th chapter for this book, which still needs to be written.

✦ ACKNOWLEDGEMENTS ✦

Writing a book reminds me of the old saying about success: it is always a matter of 10 per cent inspiration and 90 per cent perspiration. That goes for this book just as much. Writing a book is also about teamwork for me. Therefore I am very grateful to Nina Vermaesen and Jo De Brabandere for their assistance with the research and editing for both the Dutch and the English versions of this book. Without their commitment this book would have remained a vague project. I should also not forget to mention the team of BBDO Think and the management of BBDO in Brussels for their support and inspiring insights.

I would like to thank furthermore all the marketing, communications, media and brand managers that I have spoken to and consulted on the concept and the final outline of the book. They came up with refreshing ideas, challenging views and inspirational conversations. I apologize for not mentioning them personally, but one always risks forgetting someone. But I will never forget them for all of their support.

There is one person I would nevertheless like to mention more explicitly and that is Thierry Van Zeebroeck. Thierry is a true advertising and media man (I dare not say 'mad man') who has worked for some of the largest and most creative advertising agencies in the world and has been running VAR media house in Brussels for many years now. Thierry is the man who has driven the idea for this book forward.

Many thanks also to Luc Suykens and Stephan Loerke for their enthusing forewords to this book. It always feels good to read and learn from these experienced marketing and advertising professionals.

I would also like to thank Hilde Van Mechelen and Peter Saerens at Lannoo Campus, my editors for the original Dutch version of this book, and the team at Kogan Page (Paul Milner, Nancy Wallace and their colleagues) for their support and belief in the power of a book in the 21st century.

Last but not least, I would like to dedicate this book to my wife, Majella, and children, Janoushka and Jules. It was not always easy for them to live with (or next) to a writer. I should promise them once more that this is my final book (at least for the time being).

And to all of you, enjoy!
Fons

✤ **Introduction** ✤
The era of major transition

Advertising has been an important economic and social factor for over a century. It contributes substantially to economic growth and value creation. Advertising is one of the pillars of the modern consumer society, driven by brand symbolism.[1,2,3,4]

The key message of a new study from the UK Advertising Association and Deloitte (2013) is that the economic role of advertising is much broader than is usually captured. For instance, they reveal that for every £1 spent on advertising, £6 is generated for the UK economy. Advertising spend is, according to Deloitte's conclusions, a cause of economic growth rather than an effect of it.[5] Just like any other form of marketing communication, advertising is generally considered to be the key lever for brands to reach, sell to and retain consumers. But brands are facing five major challenges today:

- ✤ the rise of digital media;
- ✤ the increasing disloyalty of consumers;
- ✤ the decreasing confidence in brands;
- ✤ the advance of price-driven private label brands;
- ✤ the growing public irritation with advertising.

At the same time, more questions are emerging about the commercial effectiveness and social justification of advertising.

The digital revolution

The digital revolution presents unseen challenges for advertising as a mass medium. This is not new. Advertising form and content have both changed dramatically in recent times, often as a result of technological advancements.[6]

In the course of history, there are five major periods marked by technological innovations that have led to transformations in the field of advertising. In the early years of printed press (newspapers and magazines), advertising was largely product-oriented. Long advertising copy primarily tried to convince people by using arguments (1890–1910). The advent of radio and cinema, the breakthrough of photography and the possibilities of colour printing prompted a wave of symbolism in advertising. Advertising became form, design and seduction (1920–1940). After World War II, the breakthrough of television as a mass medium led to the growing importance of personalities and lifestyles in advertising. Those were the days of the 'mad men' (1950–1960). After that, advertising became much more driven by market segmentation, thanks to societal fragmentation and the rise of database technologies. CNN and MTV set the tone for 'narrow casting' (1970–1990). The emergence of the personal computer and the (mobile) internet has triggered the current digital revolution. Consumers have never been as empowered as they are today. This latest rapid technological change poses new challenges for advertising and advertisers, not only in terms of form, but also of content. Interactivity, participation and transparency are the new mantras. For advertising, this is the age of collaboration and connectedness.[7,8,9,10]

ZenithOptimedia expected the internet to become the world's second biggest ad medium, behind TV, in 2013. And they also expect it to keep rising.[11]

> Advertising form and content is very much determined by the main technology used in a certain era. The history of advertising knows five major technological waves. The rise of the internet and social media is pushing advertising towards a model of collaboration and connectedness between consumers and their environment.
>
> (Source: Leiss, Kline and Shally, 1997)

TABLE 0.1   Five technological waves in advertising history

Period	Technology	Type of advertising
Pre-1930	Printed press	Product
1930–1940	Radio/photography	Product symbolism
1950–1960	TV	Personalization
1970–1980	Database (MTV–CNN)	Lifestyle
1990–present	Internet	Cooperation

However, these new technologies never create radical fault lines. Instead, they initiate a process of transformation.[12] Throughout history, the arrival of a new technology has never meant the end of an existing technology. Television did not mean the end of radio as a medium. History is like the rapids on a river, constantly moving forward and constantly gaining speed. Yet history never returns. The clock cannot be turned back. It is not a question of 'business as usual'.

In essence, the business model of new digital media such as Google and Facebook can be reduced to a traditional advertising model. Services are delivered to consumers free of charge and financed by advertising income. Google generates 95 per cent of its revenue from different forms of advertising. Likewise, Facebook gets 84 per cent of its financing from advertisements (according to financial statements for the second quarter of 2012). If Facebook wants to deliver on the high expectations of its investors (the 2012 IPO failed), it will have to become, more than ever before, an advertising sales house. Paradoxical as it may seem to some, the future of Facebook and other similar sites is called 'advertising'.

At the same time, advertising's financial model is also an essential pillar of the traditional media industry. A potential implosion of the advertising model will lead to a poorer offer, as well as a decrease in quality and, ultimately, a more restricted consumer freedom of choice. In 2012, respected print brands including *Newsweek*, *Frankfurter Rundschau* and the German edition of the *Financial Times* all disappeared. Over the last five years, 268 newspaper titles are said to have vanished in the United States alone.

The disloyal consumer

Despite clear efforts from brands to invest in better customer service, overall consumer dissatisfaction is growing rapidly all over the world. This is one of the sobering conclusions from research carried out by Accenture in 2011 amongst more than 10,000 consumers about their behaviour in relation to 10 different industries (including telecommunications, banking, retail and airlines).[13] This research indicates that, compared to 2008, consumers are generally more satisfied about the customer service offered by companies, but at the same time they change brands more frequently and are constantly on the lookout for better deals. Consumers get particularly frustrated by brands that do not keep their promises. Hence, it is no surprise that customer brand disloyalty continues to increase: 66 per cent of customers worldwide said that they had changed brands because of a bad customer experience. In 2012, almost 900,000 families in Flanders made the switch to a different energy provider.

According to the Accenture study, almost one in four consumers considers him- or herself to be brand loyal. Yet just as many respondents consider themselves not to be loyal at all. It seems likely that the economic crisis has intensified this tendency, as has the rise of the internet and social media. More than ever, the consumer is in the driver's seat and is leading the way for brands. The same Accenture research shows that no less than 44 per cent of global consumers indicate that they now expect more from the brands they buy than a year ago. In 2008, only 31 per cent responded in the same way. Consumer expectations appear to be rising more quickly than brands are able (or willing) to follow.

Traditional marketing models based on higher customer satisfaction to increase retention are put to the test by research papers of this kind. Over the last few years, many brands have invested primarily in their relationships with their customers, often forced by financial imperatives. Cross-selling and up-selling to existing customers guaranteed higher short-term revenues and profitability. New powerful database management systems allowed brands to measure customer profitability better than ever before. This was also a way of cutting costs, because more sales to an existing customer is more profitable in the short term than investing in the winning of new customers.

Research on brand loyalty has already shown that consumers are generally 'loyal' to a set of brands of their preference. Today, modern families have accounts at several banks, drive cars of different brands and hold loyalty cards for a number of different supermarkets and shops. Brand loyalty is more than ever a matter of shared loyalty. Moreover, brand loyalty has been decreasing over time.[14]

Lots of brands are now placing their hopes on social media to enter into dialogue with consumers. They are proud of their so-called 'fan base' (for example, on Facebook). In late 2011, research from the respected Ehrenberg-Bass Institute for Marketing Science showed that only 1.3 per cent of these self-declared 'fans' of the biggest brands in the world are actually willing to 'commit' themselves to those brands. This is even the case for so-called 'lovemarks', like Nike or Harley-Davidson. Brand loyalty no longer seems to be part of the world we live in.[15]

Furthermore, other research has shown that consumers active on online platforms are driven mainly by prizes and competitions. However, offering free services via the internet also involves a real danger of value destruction.[16] When services are being offered or promoted below their real price, consumers receive a gift they have often not asked for. Consequently, false expectations of 'free' are being created. The decline of Groupon in the United States and Europe in 2012 is a striking example. Those eating at half price in a restaurant seldom return to pay the full price.

Moreover, the contribution to the sales of brands through social media sites such as Facebook, Twitter, LinkedIn or YouTube, is very limited. An analysis of sales made on 'Black Friday' in 2012 – the day after Thanksgiving, often regarded as one of the busiest shopping days of the year in the United States – revealed that barely 0.34 per cent of buyers turned out to be 'referred' via social media. This represents a decrease of over 35 per cent compared to the year before. The largest growth came from mobile platforms, such as the iPad.[17] Even if this is only a snapshot of reality, it is still indicative of a larger trend.

The brand bubble

Meanwhile, a revolution is taking place in the relationship between brands and consumers. A few years ago, the reputed BrandAsset™ Valuator compiled by Young & Rubicam revealed that brand confidence had dropped by about 50 per cent. Scarcely one brand in four enjoyed unconditional consumer confidence.[18] This trend still continues today, in the wake of the 2008 banking crisis.

Another study conducted by Havas Media in late 2011 demonstrated that two out of every three consumers would not miss their current brand, should it disappear tomorrow. No more than 20 per cent of consumers believe that these brands actually improve their quality of life. The study concludes that brands are becoming increasingly irrelevant to consumers.[19]

Corporate reputations are in freefall as well, according to a recent reputation survey conducted by the Reputation Institute.[20] In just one year, the average reputation scores of leading companies fell. In The Netherlands, the majority of companies scored lower in 2012 than in 2011. In Germany, two-thirds of the companies quoted on the DAX stock index lost ground. In the United Kingdom, half of the 150 companies on the list saw their scores drop, while only a third improved their scores. And a similar trend is evident in the United States: only 9 per cent of the companies included in the survey saw their reputation scores increase between 2011 and 2012. This is clearly an international trend.

The underlying causes are not hard to find. In the current economic and social climate, established institutions are being increasingly questioned. This is not only true for banks, but also for companies in many industries. The gap between the corporate world as a whole and the social concerns of the public is becoming ever wider. In the eyes of the consumer/citizen, companies have all become bankers.

From the many, often diverse, surveys and studies mentioned above, it can be concluded that a new 80/20 rule has emerged in the relationship between consumers and brands. Or to be precise: a 75/20/5 rule. This means that today 75 per cent of brands have lost consumer trust, are offering substandard services, have lost their relevance and uniqueness, are not delivering on their promises, are not meeting expectations and are, in the final analysis, interchangeable. These brands are the playthings of 'zapping and shopping' consumers, who are happy to consider cheaper alternatives, often private labels. Just 20 per cent of brands still enjoy consumer confidence and can take pride in high levels of brand loyalty. These are the brands consumers embrace as 'their' brands. And a very select 5 per cent enjoy the status of a 'lovemark'. These are the brands consumers show deep feelings towards and consider to be their 'soulmates'. Brands of this kind have an unconditional following of 'fans'.[21]

Nevertheless, additional research is still needed to determine whether a modern 'Matthew effect' (the phenomenon that the rich get richer and the poor get poorer) is involved, implying that brands with substantial brand equity will be loved even more, while other brands risk falling from consumer grace altogether.

Even so, the message is already clear for the vast majority of brands. First and foremost, they will have to work on their performance and their relevance. They will also need to account more fully to consumers for what they do. Their prime mission is to satisfy customers. But they will only rise in consumer esteem when they show empathy and succeed in commanding respect. When a brand keeps its promises, its customers will be satisfied. This is an absolute requirement for a relationship based on trust. This is particularly true for products and categories built on the basis of a more functional and instrumental bond with consumers.[22]

The rise of private labels

In the past, the private labels or generic brands offered by supermarkets were primarily a way of providing the consumer with a cheaper alternative for 'A brands'. In addition, they guaranteed supermarkets a certain independence from brand manufacturers, as well as higher profit margins. Today, private labels are no longer about price. They have become an important weapon to win consumers' hearts – and cash.

Since 2008, the economic crisis has given private labels extra impetus. In difficult economic times private labels gain ground, which they rarely seem to lose afterwards. However, this is not a new trend. Some A brands were already neglecting to invest in innovation and advertising for certain product categories. And a clear correlation has been established between private-label market share in some product categories and the advertising spending of A brands. When A brands stop advertising, private labels get a free ticket to success.[23]

Meanwhile, it is clear that supermarkets are gaining more power than ever before, to such an extent that they are slowly becoming superpowers. The power balance between producer and distributor is shifting. In recent years, Belgium and The Netherlands have seen their fair share of margin battles between these two parties. Supermarkets are outgrowing their historical role in the value chain, as well as their role as a private label. They are no longer concerned with simply taking advantage of the low prices of their own brands, but are presenting themselves increasingly as fully-fledged and responsible brands in their own right. In the United States, the marketing magazine *Advertising Age* describes Walmart, the largest retailer in the country and the world, as a true 'regulator' when it comes to sustainable business practices. Walmart imposes stricter sustainability requirements on its suppliers. In addition, the company focuses more sharply on healthy food and wants to reduce sodium, fat and sugar in foodstuffs. It is also developing a sustainable product index or green brand index. In short, the distributor is taking on the role of government.[24] In this context, however, it is noticeable that Walmart has also been under fire at the same time for ousting local community life from the neighbourhoods in which it operates.

Such actions again prove that retailers have become more than the middle-men for A brands, more than Kotler's 'P for Place' in the marketing mix. They have become A brands themselves. The quality gap has long since been closed, and heavy investments are being made in brand and corporate image. Already back in 2006, supermarkets were ranked as the 'most trustworthy industry' by Belgian consumers in research carried out by Think BBDO. Depending on the source, US research also shows that one out of every three or even one out of every two consumers considers private labels to be the worthy equivalents of A brands.

The question therefore arises whether A brands still have a bright future. If they want to stay ahead of the private labels, they will not only need to be inventive in dealing with the supermarkets, which will be both competitors and allies at the same time, but will also have to focus on innovation, smart pricing strategies, branding and advertising for their own brands.

Growing irritation with advertising

Research carried out in The Netherlands in 2012 provides insights into the reasons why consumers are irritated by and seek to avoid advertising.[25]

One remarkable conclusion is that consumers get more annoyed by the quantity of bad advertising than by the overall quantity of advertising. Bad advertising makes viewers reach for the remote control during commercial breaks: 46.9 per cent of the respondents agreed with this proposition.

The levels of attention to and appreciation for advertising depend on the medium used. Surprisingly, the Dutch seem to get more annoyed by online advertising than by print advertising, including newspapers and magazines. The 'invasion of privacy' issue plays an important role here. The more consumers are concerned about their privacy, the more they will avoid advertising on a specific digital platform. In this sense, privacy seems to be a 'Catch-22' for companies like Facebook and their potential advertisers.

When it comes to irritation, the new social media do even worse than regular websites. Consumers perceive advertising on social media sites to be less informative, less credible and less entertaining than advertising on classic websites. In the main, it seems that people simply do not want to be disturbed or distracted during their conversations with friends on social media. This is understandable: social media demand higher levels of concentration from users, because they are highly participative and interactive. For this same reason, it is hard to combine social media with other media, according to the Dutch study. This possibly explains why practical experiments with a so-called 'second screen' have only captured moderate consumer attention so far.

In terms of so-called 'clutter' (a factor that reduces advertising effectiveness by causing avoidance behaviours and memory interference/impairment) a recent study by the Ehrenberg-Bass Institute[26] unveiled very similar findings as previously found for TV and radio ads. Facebook ads were better recalled when placed among fewer other ads. The research, interestingly, also found that larger brands are more immune to clutter than smaller, lesser-known brands. Thus: low-clutter environments and as little irritation as possible are crucial for the effectiveness of smaller and/or newer brands on Facebook.

Despite these findings, advertising on digital media is currently showing record growth figures. Even so, other recent research carried out by YouGov in the United States and the United Kingdom indicates that no fewer than two out of every three respondents in these countries think that advertising on all digital channels (e-mail, website, apps, etc) is excessive and annoying, as well as being a main reason not to click through. Internet advertising is proving to be the victim of its own success[27].

At the same time, consumers seem to have a very ambiguous relationship with advertising on television. Both the average irritation level and the average entertainment level are highest for TV advertising, according to the Dutch study. In addition, TV advertising generates the highest levels of word-of-mouth advertising. Compared to advertising in other media, TV ads are the most important topic of conversation among friends.

The (somewhat overly optimistic?) conclusion of the Dutch researchers is that the limit of the public's acceptance for advertising has not yet been reached, provided that the advertising is brought in an entertaining and attractive manner. This is not that same as saying that commercial breaks should be 'brightened up'. Advertising needs to be fun and captivating in itself, and not as a result of cosmetic tricks.

Notes

1   Bughin, J and Spittaels, S (2012) Advertising as an economic-growth engine, *McKinsey & Company* [Online] http://mckinsey.com/locations/Belux/~/media/Belux/final/Advertising.ashx

2   Baudrillard, J (1970) La société de consummation, *Folio Essais*

3   Debord, G (1967) La société du spectacle, *Folio Essais*

4   Elchardus, M (2002) *De Symbolische Samenleving*, Lannoo, Tielt

5   Blackie, S and Lefroy, T (2013) The advertising economy, *Admap*, February 2013, pp 44–45

6   Leiss, W, Kline, S and Shally, S (1997) *Social Communication in Advertising: Persons, products and images of well-being*, Routledge, New York

7   Van Dyck, F (2007) *Het Merk Mens*, LannooCampus/Scriptum, Tielt

8   Hinssen, P (2010) *Digitaal is Het Nieuwe Normaal*, Lannoo/Spectrum, Tielt

9   Michils, M (2010) *Open Boek*, Lannoo Campus/Business Contact, Tielt

10   Maillet, T (2006) *Génération Participation*, MM2 Editions, Paris

11   Advertising Age (2012), 31 December 2012, p 16

12   McQuail, D (2010) *Mass Communication Theory*, SAGE, London

13   Accenture [accessed 12 November 2012] The new realities of 'dating' in the digital age, *Accenture* [Online] http://accenture.com/SiteCollectionDocuments/PDF/Accenture-Global-Consumer-Research-New-Realities.pdf

14   Franzen, G and Moriarty, S (2009) *The Science and Art of Branding*, ME Sharpe, New York

15 Creamer, M [accessed 17 January 2013] Only 1% of Facebook 'fans' engage with brands, *Advertising Age* [Online] http://adage.com/article/digital/study-1-facebook-fans-engage-brands/232351

16 Kapferer, J N (2008) *The New Strategic Brand Management*, Kogan Page, London

17 IBM [accessed 12 December 2012], Black Friday Report 2012, *IBM* [Online] http://ibm.com/software/marketing-solutions/benchmark-reports/black-friday-2012.html

18 Gerzema, J and Lebar, E (2008) *The Brand Bubble: The looming crisis in brand value and how to avoid it*, Jossey Bass, San Francisco

19 Havas Media [accessed 12 December 2012] Meaningful brands for a sustainable future *Havas media* [Online] http://havasmedia.com/meaningful-brands

20 The Reputation Institute [accessed 14 December 2012] RepTrak Pulse Study, *RepTrak* [Online] http://reputationinstitute.com/thought-leadership/global-reptrak

21 Rossiter, J and Bellman, S (2012) Emotional bonding pays off, *Journal of Advertising Research*, **52** (3), pp 291–96

22 Franzen, G, op cit, p 252

23 See 16.

24 Neff, J [accessed 12 December 2012] Move over Government, Walmart's the new regulator in town, *Advertising Age* [Online] http://adage.com/article/news/move-government-walmart-s-regulator-town/149251

25 Ketelaar, P, De Clercq, I and Heuvelman, E (2012) Het reclameconsumptiedieet van de multimediale Nederlander, *Tijdschrift voor Marketing*, **4**, pp 98–102

26 Nelson-Fiels, K, Riebe, E and Sharp, B (2013) More mutter about clutter: extending empirical generalizations to Facebook, *Journal of Advertising Research*, **53** (2), pp 186–91

27 YouGov, Upstream (2012) Digital advertising attitudes report pp18 [online] http://cache.upstreamsystems.com/wp-content/uploads/research/research_2012-DA-attitudes_report.pdf

❖ PART ONE ❖
The essence of advertising today

01

What is effective advertising?

Everybody has an opinion about advertising. That should come as no surprise, since advertising is omnipresent in our lives. Some embrace advertising as an inextricable part of our popular culture, putting the individual's freedom of choice first. Others are radically opposed and believe advertising is destroying our world. But what makes advertising effective today?

Companies continue to invest massively in advertising: about US $497 billion (382 billion euros) in 2012, or 3.3 per cent more than in 2011. This represents about the size of the gross domestic product (GDP) of a Western country like Belgium. The biggest investment in advertising per capita is made in Switzerland ($744 per person), followed by Norway ($602 per person), Australia ($580 per person) and the United States ($512 per person). For 2013, global ad spending was expected to rise by 4 per cent.[1,2]

Advertising is not new – evidence of its use can be found in Ancient Egyptian, Greek and Roman times. Yet even today, the discussion about how advertising works, what its role and return is for brands and companies continues to be a hot topic in and outside scientific circles:

✦ What is the current state of play?

✦ How does advertising *really* work?

✦ What is the difference between advertising, sales promotion and word of mouth?

❖ Does advertising need to focus on loyal customers or on 'new' customers?

❖ What are the short- and long-term effects for brands?

The advertising paradox

New neuroscientific and psychological evidence has brought fresh insights into how our brains work and how advertising works in our brains. Advertising creates memories and recalls them, working on a less conscious and emotional level than was traditionally thought. This is one of the insights presented by marketing authority Byron Sharp in his book[3] *How Brands Grow: What marketers don't know* (2010), in which he focuses on a number of important advertising topics.

Professor Sharp is the Director of the renowned Ehrenberg-Bass Institute for Marketing Science at the University of South Australia. This centre has been conducting fundamental research on how advertising works for many years, including research commissioned by global brands such as Coca-Cola, Procter & Gamble and Mars. Advertising has one purpose only, says Sharp, and that is to influence consumers' buying behaviour. More specifically, the billions of dollars that are invested in advertising every year need to stimulate and protect the sale of brands. This is an idea that will make quite a number of marketers shiver, since it conjures up associations of 'sales' or 'super promotions', whereas they prefer concepts such as 'brand value' or 'customer loyalty'. According to Sharp these notions will make the average CEO or financial director more wary than the hard sales numbers.

Sharp argues that there is sufficient empirical evidence to show that advertising leads to sales. But the effects of advertising are hard to notice in sales trends. He sees two main reasons why sales figures do not jump immediately when advertising starts, or drop immediately when advertising stops. The first reason is that most advertising simply ensures that brands can maintain their market share. First and foremost, advertising is intended to prevent sales from dropping, or else it must hinder competitors from luring customers away. This may seem like turning the world on its head, but it is thanks to advertising that brands can keep up their sales volumes. Advertising is sometimes compared to the engine of a plane that makes sure that the plane – representing sales figures – does not lose altitude. A second reason is that advertising effects on sales are only visible over a longer period of time, unless the campaign in question involves very large and concentrated efforts. For smaller companies, however, it is possible to witness short-term advertising effects. Investments in advertising for these types of companies are relatively larger compared to other marketing efforts. Their sales depend less on word-of-mouth advertising, presence in stores or effects from previous advertising.

So advertising works – but it is hard to tell just by looking at the sales figures. As a result, it is not an easy story to sell. It is made even more difficult, as Sharp suggests, by the fact that even when there is a change in sales figures, it is not certain that this is an indication of a 'real' effect. When you see the tip of the iceberg, you don't know how big the iceberg actually is, he concludes.

The importance of the light buyer

Advertising only works when it reaches the right target group. A target group that is, on the one hand, 'inclined' to buy and, on the other hand, large enough to make the difference and to ensure that advertising efforts are cost-efficient.

Every brand has different types of consumers or buyers. The literature often makes the distinction between 'heavy buyers', lovers that buy the brand several times a week, and 'light buyers', consumers that buy a brand a few times a year at best. At first sight, these heavy buyers seem the most interesting group for marketers. Not only do they buy their brand often and know it better, but frequently they also act as 'fans' of the brand on social media and in surveys, performing as true brand ambassadors.

But Sharp puts the theory of the Pareto optimum into perspective. This is a classic theory used by marketers, which assumes that 80 per cent of brand sales are realized by 20 per cent of the customer base. Based on his research, Sharp concludes that, in practice, this 80/20 rule seldom applies for many brands and in many product categories. About half of the brand sales can be attributed to light buyers, consumers that only buy the brand in question sporadically. Sharp, and with him quite a number of marketers, believes that successful advertising campaigns have to reach a broad group of consumers.

Obviously, this is the case for brands aiming for a significant market share, but not for brands entering niche markets.

Advertising needs to reach not only the group of loyal and regular customers, but also (and especially) the large group of customers that will most probably not buy the advertised brand in the coming week or month. Advertising will influence the memory structures of light buyers in such a way that they will better remember the brand when they are about to make a purchase. In these cases, advertising increases the probability that this light buyer will buy a product.

ZenithOptimedia's Touchpoints ROI Tracker research, based on interviews with over 700,000 consumers in 47 countries, dug deeper into the empirical generalization of brand recall and published its findings in the *Journal of Advertising Research* in June 2013. The research showed that – for marketers who want to reach out to all their category consumers through paid, owned and earned media – paid media have a greater potential to reach non- or light buyers, whereas owned and earned media have greater fraction among existing, thus heavy, buyers. Also, users of brands (aka heavy buyers) have a higher propensity to recall brands they use than light buyers. On average, heavy-buyer recall is 1.7 times higher than light-buyer recall.[4]

Sharp's research also confirms that, in particular, a penetration strategy aimed at reaching potential customers contributes more to brand growth than a frequency strategy, especially in the context of higher price sensitivity amongst consumers.[5] Neglecting light buyers and non-buyers is therefore not a recipe for sustainable brand growth. Campaigns based on a penetration strategy turn out to be more effective, in terms of sales as well as profitability. In addition, the current buying pattern of light buyers does not offer any guarantees for their future behaviour. Only the acquisition of new customers (in particular, light buyers) ensures sustainable market share growth for a brand.

The existence of heavy buyers and light buyers also explains the difference between the impact of advertising and sales promotions. Traditionally, advertising aims at large consumer groups, heavy buyers and light buyers alike. Sales promotions are geared more specifically towards a brand's more regular or heavy buyers. As they are limited in time, promotions tend to reach only the people who decide to make a purchase from a category during the period of the promotion. Hence, sales promotion effects are visible immediately.

Yet in contrast to advertising, these effects tend not to last beyond the period of the sales promotion. In practice, consumers return to their pre-promotion buying behaviour once the price promotion has finished. Moreover, sales promotions are expensive for a brand, since they create larger margins for retailers and consumers. Finally, the danger exists that after a sales promotion, consumers will no longer be so willing to pay the full price again. In this way, sales promotions often clear a path for discount brands and supermarket private label – generic – brands.

In summary, Sharp argues that advertising's primary purpose is to increase the market share of companies in the long term and to maintain sales in the short term. It works mainly by creating and refreshing memories and by building brand salience – the fact that a brand means something or is known by the consumer. This is particularly important in the battle to win over light buyers to a brand. These are the people who seldom or never buy the brand, yet they are a key group of potential buyers. A penetration strategy aimed at winning new customers is therefore more rewarding in the longer run than a frequency strategy aimed at heavy buyers.

TABLE 1.1   Advertising vs sales promotion

	Short term	Long term
Heavy buyers	Sales promotion	–
Light buyers	–	Advertising

Advertising is most effective when it aims at so-called 'light buyers' and works mainly in the long term. Short-term effects are created by various forms of price promotion focused on so-called 'heavy buyers'. They have a very temporary impact.

(Source: Sharp, 2010)

Direct and indirect effects of advertising

While advertising is intended to generate more sales for brands primarily via light buyers, the search for loyal customers plays a central role in other marketing models. These loyal customers ('fans') attract other customers through word of mouth and recommendations. This is a phenomenon that has grown more important with the rise of social media and the possibilities to 'share' and 'like' information via networks.

One approach that puts loyal customers first is the much-discussed Net Promoter Score (NPS) and its corresponding relationship marketing model, proposed by Fred Reichheld of the management consultancy Bain & Company. This approach is based on the central and simple question: 'How likely is it that you would recommend company x to a friend or colleague?' By its own account, NPS is the 'single most reliable indicator of a company's ability to grow'. And it is indeed used by a number of leading companies.[6]

NPS believers assume that successful companies owe their success to 'promoters', loyal customers who recommend companies and products to other, more occasional customers, amongst others things via word of mouth and the internet. Often, celebrities are mobilized to convey the same message. Some advocates even say that companies with a high NPS do not need classic advertising.

This camp of believers sees a strong increase in the importance of word-of-mouth advertising and its influence on consumers. The key reasons for this, they say, are firstly the fact that people do not trust advertising anymore, but prefer to listen to what others, especially friends, say about companies and brands. Research conducted by Nielsen seems to corroborate this.[7] In 2012, 92 per cent of consumers worldwide claimed to trust the recommendations of people they know, while half of them (47 per cent) trusted television or magazine advertising, and only a third (33 per cent) trusted online bannering. In addition, word-of-mouth advertising has the advantage of personal contact, while advertising is generally more impersonal. Conversely, word-of-mouth advertising is less controllable and adjustable, so that it can sometimes turn against the brand as well. In word-of-mouth advertising, there is said to be more 'noise'.

Practice and research show that brand advertising has a direct and indirect influence on the end consumer. In this respect, the '2-step-flow' communication model of influencing people and consumers seems to be more relevant than ever. First developed by the authoritative US sociologists Paul Lazarsfeld and Elihu Katz back in the 1950s (*Personal Influence*, 1955) this model puts forward the idea that, when forming an opinion, people are influenced by opinion-leaders, who in turn are influenced by mass media. Any social group is typically composed of 10 per cent opinion-leaders and 90 per cent opinion-followers.

Classic advertising is said to be primarily important for its ability to influence what these opinion-leaders ('promoters') think and say about the brand. In turn, these promoters then influence a broader audience.

FIGURE 1.1   2-step-flow of advertising

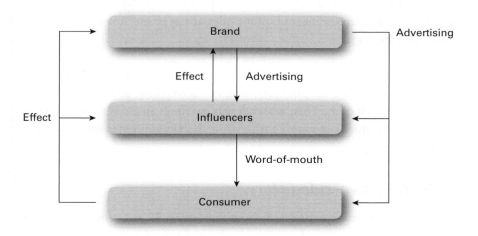

Advertising works according to a so-called '2-step-flow' model. Brand advertising reaches the consumer directly via mass media, but also indirectly through opinion-leaders. They have a word-of-mouth effect on the consumer. Ninety per cent of all conversations about brands occur in people's daily contacts, while only 10 per cent of the conversations are held via social media.

(Source: Lazarsfeld and Katz 1955[8])

A number of recently published research papers on the relationship between mass media and word-of-mouth advertising seem to confirm the validity of the 2-step-flow model. Researchers Jeffrey Graham and William Havlena published the results of their research into the impact of classic advertising on word of mouth, web searches and site visits in the *Journal of Advertising Research* in December 2007.[9]

Over a period of 26 weeks, they analysed the statistically relevant data of 35 brands in 5 different product categories, including automobile, retail, soft drinks, technology and travel. This included data on positive word of mouth, online brand mentions, advertising spending, search queries and website visits. In the first place, the results of their research confirm that word of mouth (or brand advocacy) and advertising both play an important and complementary role in building lasting relationships with consumers. They also confirm that advertising in different media can indeed generate positive word of mouth. This proves that marketers can intensify their efforts to generate word of mouth through classic advertising. The research likewise shows that offline advertising can drive online consumer behaviour, such as searches, web visits and online word of mouth. This leads to the conclusion that companies need to further gear their online and offline advertising to one another within an integrated strategy.

Research conducted by the Keller-Fay Group, published in June 2009 in the *Journal of Advertising Research*, confirms that advertising and word of mouth complement each other. Their research was based on an analysis of empirical data in 15 product categories gathered in the United States over a 3-year period.[10]

'It is still a two-sided story.'

The numbers that were analysed show that about 20 per cent of the word of mouth about brands refers to paid advertising as the source of information. In addition, the research indicates that word of mouth attributable to advertising is of a higher quality and is more likely to involve a recommendation to buy the brand. The researchers consider their conclusions to be a confirmation of the 2-step-flow model by Lazarsfeld and Katz (1955). At the same time, they pose the question whether or not advertising that is more specifically aimed at generating word of mouth could be better able to increase the effectiveness and reach of that word of mouth than traditional campaigns focused on awareness and persuasion. It is in this context that the rise of so-called 'viral advertising' – professionally made commercials that are shared via social media, particularly via YouTube, by consumers all around the world – should be considered.

Furthermore, the research carried out by Keller and Fay (2009) indicates that 'true' or 'face-to-face' word of mouth has a more powerful effect on sales than online word of mouth, especially when the influencer is standing right next to the consumer in the shop. In fact, face-to-face word of mouth has up to four times more impact than online word of mouth. Based on six years of data collection in the United States, the Keller and Fay research shows that 90 per cent of all influential conversations are still taking place in the real world. In other words, no less than 9 out of every 10 conversations about brands, companies and products are still happening in bars, in coffee corners, on the train, at the dinner table and in stores – ergo, not on Facebook or Twitter!

Another study, a 10-year US behavioural study no less, also confirms the statement that social media is not the mass-marketing tool that brands hoped for. In fact, only 11 per cent of all 1.1 million respondents say they 'regularly get or give advice' of any sort, no matter how shared. What's more, despite the rise of the internet as a medium, this percentage has not increased over the past few years.[11]

Some marketers do not seem to grasp that there is a fundamental difference between an online contact and an authentic contact in the real world. Social influence determines just about every decision people make and that influence is therefore strongest when it occurs face to face. Emotions and non-verbal language are and remain stronger than mere words.

Keller and Fay also observe that – in an era when marketing budgets are moving more and more towards online and social media – the key to success is still to strive for a balanced marketing mix. Above all, a mix aimed at light buyers. Traditional media continue to play a crucial role in stimulating conversations about brands, companies and products. In other words, it is still a two-sided story.

Professor Jenni Romaniuk, a colleague of Byron Sharp at the Ehrenberg-Bass Institute for Marketing Science, conducted additional research in 2010, 2011 and in 2012 on the impact of word-of-mouth advertising. She clarifies that research to date has put the target groups of word-of-mouth and traditional advertising in the same box. According to her, these target groups are not the same at all.[12]

The results of Romaniuk's research show that positive word of mouth primarily reaches people who already have a high predisposition to act favourably towards the brand. She also implies that traditional advertising has more impact on the behaviour of the undecided members of the target group. The reason for this is that the 'traditional advertising audience' has more 'room for change' in their behaviour. In addition, traditional advertising has the advantage of being able to potentially reach a wider audience (of undecided people), according to Romaniuk. Audiences reached by TV, gift-packs, in-store displays and outdoor ads closely matched light buyers' profiles. Most other media leaned towards heavy buyers, especially positive word of mouth and social media.[13]

Fans or followers on social media are primarily heavy buyers, ie not the light buyers brands need first and foremost in order to grow in a sustainable way.

What are Facebook fans really worth?

Now that social media are breaking through as new platforms for brands to reach their consumers, the discussion about the role of advertising and reaching the right target groups is growing increasingly important. When a brand is able to gather a large number of fans on social media, it is self-evident that brands can reach those fans easily with specific messages and should therefore be able to convince them to buy.

In June 2012, Karen Nelson-Field, Erica Riebe and Byron Sharp of the Ehrenberg-Bass Institute for Marketing Science published a remarkable piece of research about the potential reach towards a Facebook fan base, compared to the existing buying bases of two fast-moving consumer goods (FMCG) brands.[14]

Typically, the success of marketing efforts on social media such as Facebook is measured on the basis of the number of fans they were able to generate. But how valuable are these fans for brands, in terms of buying behaviour? Are Facebook fans heavy or light buyers, and what is the concentration of these different consumer profiles within the total fan base?

What truly determines consumer loyalty?

According to a survey about brand loyalty amongst US internet users, the best ways to build consumer brand loyalty are:

❖ providing exceptional 24/7 customer service (34 per cent);

❖ rewarding purchases and feedback (20 per cent);

❖ exclusive and/or relevant offers and specials (13 per cent);

❖ personalized products and services (12 per cent);

❖ knowing the customer when he or she visits or calls in (10 per cent).

(**SOURCE** Garcia, K (2012) Social Loyalty: From rewards to a rewarding customer experience, eMarketer, June 2012 (consulted online))

The Ehrenberg-Bass Institute team compared data about the profile of the Facebook fan base with that of the total typical customer base of two FMCG brands (chocolate and soft drink) in terms of buying behaviour. The results were remarkable. The Facebook fan base was very different from, if not completely opposite to, the typical customer base of both the chocolate and the soft-drink brand. While the share of non-buyers and light buyers in the typical customer base amounted to 80 to 90 per cent, this share only averaged 13 per cent in the Facebook fan base. Conversely, the typical customer base of both brands showed a small minority of heavy buyers, while in the case of the Facebook fan base, this share of heavy buyers amounted to an average of 60 per cent.

A second test was conducted to validate the earlier findings. The Facebook fan base profile was compared to the 2012 Super Bowl viewing audience. While a little less clear-cut, the results were comparable to those based on the typical buying base.

The researchers conclude that Facebook offers advertisers a platform that is aimed primarily at heavy buyers, but gives them little access to the light buyers, particularly if the desired outcome of communication efforts is to grow the brand. Their research also confirms that both newer and older Facebook fans turn out to be heavy buyers, so that their profile does not appear to change over time.

The somewhat controversial final conclusion drawn by the researchers is that the value of Facebook as a stand-alone earned advertising medium is open to question. As part of a media mix reaching the missing light buyers, the choice for a platform such as Facebook could be justified. However, the researchers query whether it is cost-efficient to include a medium that is primarily aimed at heavy buyers. According to Sharp and his team, the largest benefit of a Facebook fan base is that it can offer brands a forum to listen to heavy buyers, in order to gain new insights. In addition, they see the potential for a social network such as Facebook to turn fans into brand advocates, creating new networks that include light buyers.

In their article, Sharp and his colleagues again plead the case for the importance of the light buyer. In advertising strategy, they argue, it is not important how much a consumer buys, but how that consumer responds to advertising. Heavy-loyal customers may well be worth more to the brand per customer, but can advertising stimulate them to buy even more than they do already? They contend that the ideal medium, or media mix, reaches all potential buyers within a product category, so that both the heavy buyers and the light buyers and possibly even interested non-buyers can be addressed. It is certainly easier to reach the heavy buyer with advertising, since he or she is more receptive to advertisements and other brand marketing efforts. But reaching the light buyer is the real challenge and is also more valuable to the advertiser – or so the researchers conclude.

Summary

The primary purpose of advertising is to stimulate and maintain the sale of products and brands. Advertising is particularly successful when it reaches a wide target group, consisting mainly of light buyers.

The impact of sales promotions is limited in time and increases the chance of brand disloyalty. Advertising has a direct impact on consumers as well as an indirect impact, via word of mouth, conversations about brands and campaigns. In this case, advertising generates a snowball effect from influencers to the individual consumer. The majority of conversation about brands still occurs in real life and not on social media.

Practical inspiration

1 What is the share of heavy buyers and light buyers in your brand sales?

2 What is the evolution in market share of private labels and discount brands in your market and what strategy are you using?

3 Do you know your brand's influencers and how to reach them proactively?

4 Weigh the pros and cons of a penetration and a frequency strategy for your brand.

5 How many Facebook fans does your brand have and what more do they do than click the 'like' button?

CASE STUDY   Nike: 'Find Your Greatness'

After years and years of 'just doing it', Nike went beyond its sports category. With 'Find Your Greatness', the sports brand wanted to show that if you have a body, you are an athlete too. Nike thus opted for a new approach by inspiring everyday people aka 'light buyers' to 'start moving'. The 2012 Olympics in London provided the perfect setting: the whole world was looking on as the sports brand chose to focus on the millions of 'regular' people, challenging the conventions of greatness in the 'real' world. As a result, Nike had the most talked-about campaign during the Games, driving a phenomenal $506 million in revenue growth. And it did indeed get people moving again, increasing Nike+ membership by 55 per cent. The reward was a Silver North American Effie in 2013.

SOURCE Effie Worldwide (2012). Nike. Find your greatness. Consulted online: www.effie.org

Notes

1   Bradley, J (2012) 100 Largest global marketers 2012, *Advertising Age*, 10 December, pp 16–18

2   Annual Report (2013) 31 December, p 32

3   Sharp, B (2010) *How Brands Grow: What marketers don't know*, Oxford University Press, New York

4   Harrison, F (2013) Digging deeper down into the empirical generalization of brand recall: adding owned and earned media to paid-media touchpoints, *Journal of Advertising Research*, **53** (2), pp 181–85

5   Franzen, G and Moriarty, S (2009) *The Science and Art of Branding*, ME Sharpe, New York, pp 327–28

6   Reichheld, F (2011) *The Ultimate Question 2.0*, Harvard Business Review Press, Boston

7   Nielsen [accessed 26 December 2012] Global Trust in advertising and Brand Messages, *Nielsen* [Online] http://nielsen.com/us/en/reports/2012/global-trust-in-advertising-and-brand-messages.html

8   Lazarsfeld and Katz (1955) *The Personal Influence*, Transaction Publishers

9   Graham, J and Havlena, W (2007) Finding the 'missing link': advertising's impact on word of mouth, web searches and site visits, *Journal of Advertising Research*, **47** (4), pp 427–35

10   Keller, E and Fay, B (2012) *The Face-to-Face Book: Why real relationships rule in a digital marketplace*, Free Press, New York

11   Schultz, D E (2013) Social Media: Friend or foe? *Admap*, May 2013, pp 22–23

12   Romaniuk, J [accessed 16 November 2012] Advertising Is More Influential Than Word Of Mouth? That would be something to talk about! *WARC Advertising Research Foundation* [Online] http://anzmac.org/conference/2011/Papers%20by%20Presenting%20Author/Romaniuk,%20Jenni%20Paper%20325.pdf

13   Romaniuk, J, Beal, V and Uncles, M (2013) Achieving reach in a multi-media environment. How a marketer's first step provides the direction for the second, *Journal of Advertising Research*, 53 (2), pp 221–30

14   Nelson-Field, K, Riebe, E and Sharp, B (2012) What's not to 'like'? Can a Facebook fan base give a brand the advertising reach it needs? *Journal of Advertising Research*, 52 (2), pp 262–69

02

The advertising
ecosystem

The world today, in particular the world of advertising, is becoming increasingly characterized by fragmentation. As time passes, consumers are becoming more and more empowered and expect to assume a much more central role. At the same time, the needs of these consumers are growing ever more diverse, so that ever greater market segmentation is necessary. How are brands reacting to these evolutions?

The shift towards segmented marketing is also being accelerated by the rapid developments in information technology. With current IT applications, marketers are able to follow and meet the needs of consumers more closely.[1]

To deal effectively with this segmentation and to ensure that investments are made efficiently, the need for a holistic approach to advertising is more urgent than ever before. This must go much further than the integration of marketing communication. After all, consumers make little or no distinction between the different sources of advertising. The messages from different media, such as television, magazines and online channels, are simply merged in the consumer's mind. Together with the messages projected by the different sales promotions, they are compressed into a single total message about the brand or company.

Always in motion

Within the framework of the international Advertising Research Foundation (ARF), in the winter of 2010 the so-called '360 Media and Marketing Super Council' developed a theoretical model for an integrated media and marketing approach. There is a consensus amongst the members of the council that there is no such thing as a static model for integrated marketing communication. Instead, they prefer to speak of an 'always-in-motion ecosystem'. This is a circular model in which there is no starting point and no finishing point, so that all the different component circles – or spheres – are of equal value and relevance.[2]

The important thing about this model is that 'the human' – and not 'the consumer' – is at its centre. This was a conscious decision by the council, intended as a signal to the industry that consumption is only a part of people's lives. According to the council, in modern marketing it is necessary for the industry to react to the choices that consumers make – and not the other way around.

Nowadays, people are much more complex than in the past, often filling a number of different roles in society. The same person might be a consumer, citizen, employee or even a shareholder. He or she still wishes to satisfy his or her own needs as a consumer, but no longer at the cost of everything else. Sustainability and social responsibility for people as citizens are becoming increasingly important and an integrated approach needs to adopt a much more holistic view that takes due account of these matters.[3]

Stakeholders and staff are also unquestionably assuming a position of increasing prominence, since both these 'roles' are crucial for translating the promises made by the brand's advertising into hard practice.

> The ARF 360° model is an 'always-in-motion' ecosystem. It is a circular model in which all the different component spheres are of equal importance. This means that there is no single starting point or finishing point: the model could be initiated from any of the spheres. The 'human' sphere is at the centre of the model. This is intended as a conscious signal to the industry, underlining the fact that consumption is only a part of people's lives. All aspects of the model touch this group. People can also set the process in motion by seeking interaction with a category or brand.
>
> (Source: Romaniuk, 2010, *Journal of Advertising Research*, 50 (3))

FIGURE 2.1   The ARF 360° model

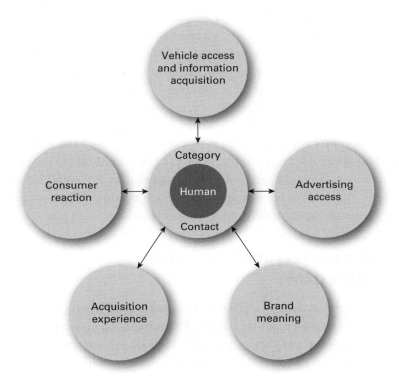

The central sphere: the human

The individual person, the human being at whom the campaign is targeted, stands in a central position, because all other parts of the model come into contact with this group. The person can also set the process in motion him- or herself, by seeking to interact with a category or brand.

There are different elements that need to be considered with regard to this central 'human' sphere. A first element relates to the so-called 'descriptive characteristics – including demographic, psychographic and behavioural attributes – which indicate who buys or could buy the brand. Account also needs to be taken of people's motives and psychological drivers – which can be many and varied – and people's different needs and wants, both within the categories and in relation to brands. There are also cultural and environmental influences, which can have an impact on people's values and how they evaluate experiences, such as their exposure to media and advertising.

Similarly, the manner in which people process advertising is equally crucial, although there are currently several different theories relating to this element. Moreover, the rapid growth of social and searchable media mean that people's engagement and involvement are becoming increasingly important, because in the different steps of the process each individual decides exactly how much effort he or she wishes to invest. Advertisers can optimize their budgets if they can gain greater insight into the levels of interaction and involvement that people want. Finally, there is the category context surrounding the human, or the lens through which the marketers and advertisers need to examine each of the other spheres, in order to better understand the way people make their decisions. For example, if the category is one where people seek information, choosing a medium that is regarded as a credible source of accessible information is more important than it would be for a category where people do not generally require information.

The vehicle access and information acquisition sphere

The second sphere of the model – vehicle access and information acquisition – represents the media mix that actually brings the campaign to the attention of the consumer; a mix that can include both traditional and new media. Every combination of vehicles, but also each vehicle in itself, has both advantages and disadvantages. Moreover, the range of media choices and options open to advertisers is now extremely complex.

Within the media sphere, there are once again several elements that need to be taken into consideration, since they each have the potential to significantly influence the advertising campaign... First and foremost, the maximum size of the target audience needs to be established. What is the total number of people that can be reached by each medium? The nature of the target audience must also be assessed. Who will be using which medium and how can you ensure that every relevant group is covered? Next, there is the pattern of media consumption, which analyses when, how often and for how long people use various media. Once again, the involvement of the consumer during his or her exposure to the medium is another important parameter. Finally, there is the capability and desirability of using certain types of media interactively (the 'push and pull' of information).

The campaign creative and scheduling sphere

This sphere represents how a campaign is created and delivered to an audience. It consists of two separate elements: the content of the advertising and how it is scheduled. Both elements have the same impact on the effectiveness of any campaign.

The content of the campaign can also be divided into four dimensions, which will determine whether or not individual members of the public will react positively to the advertising exposure. The first dimension is creative quality, which captures the essence of the advertising style and relates to the feelings and evaluations that the advertising can induce in the target public. The second dimension is context, which is a separate aspect of creative quality, expressing the extent to which the creative element is suitable for the environment in which it is being used. Next, there is the quality of the branding in the execution. This relates to the ease with which the audience can identify with the brand being advertised. Last but not least, there is also the quality of the message. Is the message persuasive and relevant? Does it contain information that is useful to the recipient?

It is against this background that the rise of 'branded content' or 'brand storytelling' needs to be understood. In this way, brands can adjust to the different contexts of their consumers by offering them tailor-made 'stories'.

The scheduling element of the advertising likewise consists of a number of different variables that can impact the overall effectiveness of the advertising exposure.

The first and most obvious factor is the reach of the campaign. How many people will see or hear it? What will be the added effect of word-of-mouth opportunities? Frequency is another important consideration. How often will people see or hear the campaign in each medium and across media? How long will it take before the campaign has outlived its usefulness (wearout)? Recent research has also demonstrated the importance of the weight of the campaign and its ability to capture a sufficiently large share of voice, since this has a key influence on both reach and frequency. Finally, the dimensions of timing – at what times of the day should the campaign be delivered – and continuity – should the campaign be ongoing or phased – must not be overlooked.

The brand history and meaning sphere

This sphere represents how the brand's past activities have accumulated in consumer memory, thereby creating a certain perception of the brand. This accumulated perception in turn influences how consumers process and react to future interactions with the brand, including its advertising.

The ARF model distinguishes five factors that need to be considered within this sphere of the advertising ecosystem:

1 *Prior brand usage* – has the consumer bought the brand in the past? Is he or she a heavy buyer or a light buyer?

2 *Level of brand awareness* – can the consumer attribute the brand to a particular category?

3 *Brand knowledge* – the sum of associations that the consumer has built up over a period of time on the basis of his or her experiences and interaction with the brand will influence response to advertising exposure.

4 *Brand salience*, or the extent to which the brand is easily noticed and accessed in purchase situations.

5 *Brand attitude, brand preference and brand engagement*, which together encapsulate the way a consumer feels about a particular brand.

The acquisition experience sphere

This sphere deals with the complete range of acquisition experiences – in-store, by phone, online, etc – and how these experiences can affect both the process and the ultimate outcome. Once again, several variable elements are at play.

One of the most important is buyer reach, or the number of people that use a particular channel, which in turn is influenced by any potential barriers to the use of that channel. Previous experience of a channel or the purchasing environment can also impact the process. For example, how much time is the consumer willing to spend on his or her purchase? Brand visibility in different sales channels is also a key factor in determining brand experience, as are promotions and special offers (point-of-sale inducements), since these often persuade wavering consumers to commit to a purchase. Nor should the importance of the nature of the purchasing decision be overlooked. Is it a new or habitual purchase? A familiar process may be more difficult to change than an irregular (or new) purchase.

The consumer reaction sphere

The final sphere represents the behavioural response to be evoked. Ideally, this response should lead to a purchase, at least according to the creators of the ARF model. But they also concede that the purpose of a campaign might be to simply encourage people to move towards a purchase at some point in the future.

In this context, several different outcomes may be sought:

✤ *Trial* – getting new users to buy the brand;

✤ *Penetration increase* – increasing the number of people who buy the brand during any time period;

✤ *Loyalty* – persuading existing customers to buy more, more often, and to remain customers;

✤ *Accelerated use* – targeting existing customers to use the brand more frequently, to reduce inter-purchase times;

✤ *Word of mouth* – having people talk about or recommend the brand to others;

✤ *Website visitation* – encouraging people to go to a website for more information or as a step towards a purchase;

✤ *Joining an online community* – this can signal greater brand commitment.

As mentioned previously, in a perfect world every road leads to a purchase by the consumer, but a campaign may just as legitimately seek to persuade the consumer to take certain measures within a specific sphere of the ecosystem.

According to its instigators, the ARF model can be used to describe the processes involved in developing and evaluating a campaign and can therefore function as a touchstone for advertisers and agencies. The ARF Council regards its model as being both sufficiently inclusive and sufficiently flexible, so that it can continue to respond, chameleon-like, to the non-stop evolutions of our ever-changing world.

AIDA and ADIA: the best of both worlds

The purpose of advertising continues to be the influencing of consumer behaviour in a particular direction. In addition to activating the consumer in this manner, it also seeks to bind him or her to the advertising brand. Here, too, an evolution towards a more holistic approach is becoming increasingly apparent.

As early as 1898 the famous US advertising pioneer Elias St Elmo Lewis, developed his AIDA model. AIDA is based on a hierarchy of effects and describes the processes that a consumer undergoes when he or she is motivated to make a purchase by external stimuli.[4] This traditional model involves a sequence of four successive steps, whose initial letters form the 'AIDA' acronym:

1 *Awareness*: the objective is to use advertising to draw the attention of potential customers to a particular product or service. The more familiar a brand is, the more likely it will feature prominently in the consumer's mental shortlist of options.

2 *Interest*: once the prospect's attention has been attracted to the brand, his or her interest needs to be stimulated by offering him or her the promise of an added value. In this way, the prospect knows what he or she has to pay and what he or she will get in return. The aim is to create a positive brand attitude.

3 *Desire*: now that the prospect is interested, this next step seeks to cement his or her commitment by answering the inherent questions posed by all consumers: 'Is this what I want, is this what I need?' If the consumer can answer 'yes' to both these questions, he or she will be prepared to make a purchase.

4 *Action*: once the desire for the product or service has been generated, the prospect is ready to take action. A hard-to-refuse promotional offer can often help to make up the mind of any purchasers who may still doubt. The aim of the brand is to secure a purchase now – not later.

This conventional – and, according to some pundits, outdated – marketing approach is based on a hierarchy of objectives and effects. The AIDA model focuses in particular on the large group of light buyers (see Chapter 1) and is intended, as mentioned previously, to persuade the consumer to make an immediate purchase.

How H&M launched a strong and integrated campaign

Advertising time during the US Super Bowl is probably the most coveted advertising time in the world. Each year the world's largest brands queue up to invest huge amounts of money and energy in these highly desirable advertising spots.

In 2012 the clothing chain H&M took out one of the spots for the very first time. Half the viewers of the Super Bowl are women, but very few advertisers target this group during what is traditionally perceived as a 'male' event. H&M saw things differently – they decided to show a 30-second commercial that consisted of little more than David Beckham wearing a pair of boxer shorts.

It was a triumph. H&M's first Super Bowl spot resulted in more than 2 million impressions within a month. The sale of the David Beckham line trebled and the standard H&M men's line also received a healthy boost in the two weeks following the game. So how did H&M achieve this success?

1   By integrating all channels (print, outdoor, online, television, etc) to project the same message via a phased approach: first teasers in print and posters, then online via YouTube, and finally the spot on television during the game.

2   By daring to move out of their comfort zone and look beyond classic categories and traditional thinking. For example, H&M also put adverts for women in well-known sports magazines, such as *Sports International.*

3   By using the right people for the right job, even if this meant new and additional recruitment. H&M had the foresight to set up a social team, which at key moments in the campaign and during the Super Bowl itself monitored all relevant online pages and interacted with the most important influencers.

4   By ensuring that the entire company was on board and fully committed to the project. In other words: by achieving integration at an organizational level. H&M is an international brand, which meant that all its relevant partners and shops around the world needed to be kept informed of what was happening, so that there would be sufficient stocks available if the advert achieved its desired effect.

5   Sex sometimes sells, especially if it is linked to celebrities!

SOURCE Taylor, H, (2012) Five things H&M learned from advertising during the Super Bowl. Consulted online http://www.ecoconsultancy.com/uk/blog/10696-five-things-h-m-learned-from-advertising-during-the-superbowl

In his book *Flip the Funnel* the influential marketing consultant Joseph Jaffe (2010) put forward an alternative model to AIDA, a model that is based more fundamentally on the use of existing customers than on traditional advertising. These customers are rewarded and empowered because of their willingness to talk about brands, which in turn attracts new customers.[5]

According to Jaffe, the move in the direction of an integrated approach is characterized by a shift away from the classic AIDA model and towards the alternative ADIA model. The hierarchy of objectives and desired effects is no longer the same as in the past, so that the traditional marketing model now needs to be reversed.

The purpose of this inverted model is no longer to encourage the customers to make a single purchase, but is instead more closely focused on increasing levels of customer retention. With this aim in mind, the ADIA model seeks to achieve the following effects, which do not necessarily need to follow each other in a linear manner:

✚ *Acknowledgement*: in this first step existing customers are acknowledged and thanked for their loyalty. Strong emphasis is placed on their importance for the company and the brand. This can be achieved with a simple 'thank-you' letter, an e-mail, an informative message accompanying the dispatch confirmation for a new order, the notification of a price reduction, etc. Alternatively, it is possible to use a polite, non-intrusive telephone call, just to check that the customer is still not experiencing problems with the brand. The purpose of this first step is to build up a strong bond with existing customers.

✚ *Dialogue*: the relationship between the customer and the company must not become faceless. On the contrary, there must be constant communication in both directions. Nowadays, it is impossible to confine all conversations about a brand to the company and the customer. Customers will inevitably talk to each other. This dialogue might not always be complimentary, and will sometimes include complaints, concerns, challenges, etc. To activate and participate in a positive dialogue, the brand needs to make the necessary social platforms available to its customers. In short, it needs to create digital communities, where customers and prospects can come into contact with each other. Once the communities have been set up and the dialogue has commenced, the brand must also be sufficiently proactive in its approach, participating in conversations when useful or necessary. It is not enough to encourage existing customers to engage in more conversations; the company must also listen, answer and offer new stimuli. This requires the striking of the right balance between smart, modern technology and the 'human touch'.

❖ *Incentivization*: loyal customers must be recognized and rewarded for their repurchases and their influence on the purchases of others. This is where traditional loyalty programmes show their limitations. Customers must be segmented on the basis of what they do for the brand, and they must be rewarded both functionally and emotionally. For this reason, this model requires less investment in traditional mass advertising but greater investment in the individual people who talk about the brand: the so-called 'influencers'. It is crucial to create a strong customer experience for these people, since this in turn creates a 'win-win' situation for all concerned: the new customer receives benefits; the influencer also receives benefits and the marketer receives new business.

❖ *Activation*: in this last step resources are mobilized to activate the collective potential of the mass of consumers. This involves an authentic collaboration between the brand and the customers to build and expand a living community. If this is managed properly, the result will be a customer-centric ecosystem that thrives on loyalty and word-of-mouth advertising. Sales will automatically follow.

In other words – at least, according to Joseph Jaffe – retention is the new acquisition. In this respect, he concurs with the believers in the NPS strategy (see Chapter 1). Customers must become fans, ambassadors who share positive experiences and positive stories about the brand with other consumers. Word-of-mouth advertising is stimulated by making it as easy as possible for them to talk about the brand.

'AIDA and ADIA are complementary models'

In this sense, the ADIA model concentrates on heavy buyers and is a modern form of loyalty programme, which has been strengthened in recent times by the growth of social media. These media are the perfect tool for brands to identify and interact with their most profitable customers.

As has been well documented, the debates about the relative merits (and demerits) of AIDA and ADIA are frequently fierce and uncompromising. It also needs to be questioned whether or not the processes for influencing consumer behaviour can be reduced to simple schedules of this kind. Nevertheless, in the final analysis the two models are not actually contradictory. On the contrary, they are complementary. Nowadays, the classic media brands are also starting to focus more heavily on the build-up and maintenance of a relationship of trust with their consumers. The rise of social and other online media make the integration between marketing and communication more necessary than ever before. It is our conviction that this integration should be strengthened first and foremost in terms of content based on a single strategy and an acquisitive creative concept. At the level of exploiting channels and resources, advertising still fulfils a central role in the impactful (large reach) positioning of the brand and guarantees its consistent performance over a longer period. It also ensures the realization of previously set objectives, particularly as far as the group of light buyers is concerned.

Research carried out by the Institute of Practitioners in Advertising (IPA) in the United Kingdom into the most successful advertising campaigns has shown that a penetration strategy, aimed at the acquisition of new customers, is significantly more profitable than a so-called loyalty strategy. A loyalty strategy only becomes more profitable if it succeeds in acquiring new customers as well; in other words, when loyal customers also recruit new customers. But it then becomes a penetration strategy by default. Expressed differently, this means that the best loyalty strategy is a penetration strategy targeted at light buyers (see Chapter 1).[6]

Thresholds

Today, however, a truly integrated approach is still more the exception than the rule. The majority of companies, brands and advertising agencies still get no further than the integration of the different channels. Thinking and acting consistently in terms of an advertising ecosystem is not an easy process and there are many obstacles confronting the advertisers and agencies that wish to try.[7]

The largest of these obstacles is found at the organizational level. The different departments in a company sharply define and defend their own territories, so that cross-disciplinary and cross-functional activities are hampered. Inter-departmental cultural differences and a lack of flexibility are the main stumbling blocks. Moreover, in the modern business world, expertise is often spread across several divisions: for instance, public relations is a very different specialization from advertising, and sales has very little in common with marketing. There are too few people with experience in all the marketing communication disciplines.

On the other side of the coin, integration can also act as a break on creativity. Ideas and concepts must fit into the 'broader picture' painted by the single overarching strategy. This requires strong coordination and control.

Time can also be a complicating factor, since the different resources do not always follow the same timeline. Classic media are more suitable for long-term image campaigns, whereas sales promotions are more focused on the short term.

Yet having said all this, the brands that can successfully achieve an integrated approach within an advertising ecosystem will certainly reap significant rewards. Integration does not have to mean stifling uniformity. It is more a matter of creating 'unity in diversity'. This is the only way for a message to provide the right answers to the questions posed by a fragmented market and volatile consumers.

Thinking and acting within the context of an advertising ecosystem can also yield a number of competitive advantages. It not only stimulates sales and profits, but also saves time, money and effort. The relevant partners no longer need to duplicate each other's work in isolation, but instead can share their knowledge and resources across the different disciplines. Integration leads to greater consistency, increased efficiency and bigger impact.

However, a recent study conducted by researchers of the Ehrenberg-Bass Institute, together with researchers of the FMCG global brand Mars, revealed that the sales effects of mixed media exposure (online and television) might not indicate the presence of a synergy in sales impact. When an online campaign is added to the typical TV campaign, much of the extra reach is duplicated and could, according to the researchers, therefore be regarded as frequency across media. Higher frequency however, typically brings extra sales with diminishing returns. Online exposure often shows a sales response, but not consistently either. Further research is clearly still needed, though: as cross-media campaigns are becoming the norm, there is still a lack of knowledge on the sales impact and with many a marketer waiting for clarification.[8]

Summary

Against the background of the increasing fragmentation of the marketing world, it has become imperative to recognize the need for greater integration. Marketers must think and act within the context of an advertising ecosystem. In this holistic approach, the human occupies the central position; much more complete than in his or her limited role as a consumer. The ARF model describes six spheres that allow the mechanisms of advertising to be better understood. It is also a stimulus towards the more efficient and effective use of resources.

Practical inspiration

1 Do you have a clear view of the different roles played by people (consumer, employee, stakeholder, shareholder) and do you relate to them in a holistic manner as a brand?

2 To what extent do the categories in which your brand is situated show specific characteristics in comparison with other sectors?

3 Is the exploitation of social media simply a way to cut costs or is it also a way to grow the brand?

4 Do you actively stimulate your loyal customers to recruit new customers? What are the positive and negative experiences?

5 How does your company organize an integrated marketing communication approach?

CASE STUDY   The Evian 'Roller Babies'

In 2009, Evian wanted to differentiate itself more clearly from its competitors in the market. To achieve this, Danone's star product decided to play the emotional card, with a return to its previous strategy of using babies (this time doing hip-hop dances on roller-skates!) and this with a total integration of media. Above and online channels were utilized to implement a phased approach with which the brand wanted both to encourage customers to purchase (AIDA) as well as increase retention (ADIA).

The results were – and remain – outstanding. In 2011 the spot was viewed no fewer than 140 million times around the world. The value-for-money perception of Evian rose by 17 points and the brand acquired (and maintains) a coherent worldwide image of health and purity. Countries such as the United Kingdom, the United States and even Japan all bought the campaign for use in their own markets. Not surprisingly – and quite rightly – in 2010, Evian was honoured with the award of a Grand Effie in France.

SOURCE Effie France (2009). Evian. Roller Babies. Consulted online: www.effie.fr

Notes

1   Kotler, P and Armstrong, G (2011) *Marketing, de Essentie*, Pearson, Benelux BV

2   Romaniuk, J (2010) The ARF 360 model: update to a human-centric approach, *Journal of Advertising Research*, **50** (3), pp 334–43

3   Van Dyck, F (2009) *Het Merk Mens*, LannooCampus/Scriptum, Tielt

4   Pringle, H and Field, P (2008) *Brand Immortality: How brands can live long and prosper*, Kogan Page, London

5   Jaffe, J (2010) *Flip the Funnel: How to use existing customers to get new ones*, John Wiley & Sons, New Jersey

6   Kitchen, P J, Brignell, J, Li, T and Jones, G S (2004) The emergence of IMC. A theoretical perspective, *Journal of Advertising Research*, **44** (1), pp 19–30

7   Kliatchko, J (2008) Revisiting the IMC construct. A revised definition and four pillars, *International Journal of Advertising*, **27**(1), pp 133–63

8   Taylor, J *et al* (2013) Is the multi-platform whole more powerful than its separate parts? Measuring the sales effects of cross-media advertising, *Journal of AdvertisingResearch*, **5** (2), pp 200–211

03

Creativity is king

Although the importance of creativity in advertising is generally recognized, within the advertising industry itself and within the agency-advertiser relationship there is still considerable discussion about the degree, if any, to which this creativity actually contributes towards the effectiveness of a campaign. What is it that actually makes millions of people around the world watch and share advertising films, and this at a moment in time when irritation with advertising has never been greater?

As far as this discussion is concerned, the very least that can be said is that there is no agreement about precisely what constitutes creative advertising. Is 'creative' the same as 'being original' or 'attracting people's attention', or are there other factors at play? Creativity is not a clearly defined concept. *The Oxford Dictionary* defines it as 'the use of imagination or original ideas to create something'.[1]

Bad advertising can cost lots of money

If you look at the different elements in an advertising campaign, more than three-quarters of that campaign's success is often dependent upon the style and the content of the advertisement itself. This should not be confused with the importance of the product's performance, which is even more important for the success of sales, but as far as the decisions about advertising and media planning are concerned, creativity is king. Advertisers need to make powerful adverts, if they want to make money from their expensive media plans. I cannot emphasize the importance of this strongly enough.

This, at least, is the opinion of the Canadian expert in advertising research, John Hallward, who works for the Ipsos ASI market research bureau. He has been collecting data about the mechanisms of advertising for 30 years in more than 60 different product categories.[2]

In his book *Gimme!*, (2007) Hallward explores the importance of creativity in advertising in more depth. In general, the making of advertisements costs about a fifth of the total advertising budget, with the purchase of media space gobbling up the rest. But ironically, according to Hallward, three-quarters of the success of a campaign is actually dependent upon the quality of the advertisement itself.

Advertising must work well from the very beginning of the campaign – and Hallward argues that creativity is the key. Data from the Ipsos ASI Ad* Graph Tracking Databank suggests that good advertising makes the break-through immediately and remains fixed in the memory of the target public (good recall). In terms of efficiency, media exposure can never compensate for a badly made and non-creative campaign. Brands that fail to correct or withdraw bad campaigns promptly will find themselves paying a small fortune for media space that yields them little or no return. Hallward offers figures which show that creativity works best in advertising when it is used in the context of a uniform creative platform, applied consistently in all the different channels and resources employed in the campaign (concept transfer). When a campaign makes use of different creative approaches or messages for each different channel or resource, this fragmentation results in a less effective campaign. Hence the need for integration, within the framework of 'unity in diversity' (see Chapter 2).

Creative advertising enhances brand recall

One of the most common complaints about the effect of creative advertising is that the attention given to the creative ad actually draws attention away from the merits of the brand being advertised. It is similarly argued that even if creative advertising does have a positive effect on the consumer, this effect diminishes when the consumer becomes more familiar with the ad in question.

In 2002, researchers Rik Pieters, Luc Warlop and Michel Wedel of the Universities of Tilburg, Leuven and Groningen investigated whether the originality and familiarity of advertising has an effect on the attention that consumers give to the advertising brand and their ability to remember that brand. They used an infrared technique to track the eye fixation of 119 respondents in relation to the brand, text and images of 58 page-size advertisements. The test was supplemented with a further memory test, which required the respondents to associate particular brands with particular ads.[3]

The researchers took as their starting point the idea that most consumers experience the originality of an advertisement in a similar way and that this originality is not determined by a single creative technique. A panel of students made the selection of the original advertisements. These were 'everyday' ads that had appeared in magazines. The results of the research showed that the originality of an ad – which is how they interpret creativity – can have a positive effect on brand recall in two different ways. Firstly, there is a direct effect: the consumer devotes more attention to the brand in original advertise-ments, which leads to the better memorization of information about that brand. This positive effect is even stronger for original ads, which give the consumer the feeling that he or she has already seen them before. The second effect is more subtle. Originality combined with familiarity – having seen the advertisement before – increases the ability of the consumer to call up information about the brand from his or her memory. In other words, original ads 'stick' longer in the mind of the viewer.

The researchers concluded from these results that 'originality' in advertising can be useful for campaigns that are aimed in the first instance at increasing brand awareness. They stressed that their research made no attempt to specifi-cally assess matters such as brand attitude and brand associations. They further added that in their opinion increased attention is a necessary condition for an effective advertising campaign, but by no means the only one.

The US researchers Brian Till and Daniel Baack (2005) took things a stage further, not only investigating the effect of creative advertising on brand recall, but also assessing attitudes and purchase intention with respect to those brands.[4]

'Creative advertising is more easily recalled'

In their first two studies, Till and Baack examined whether the respondents were better able to remember 'creative' ads and their brands (the sample consisted of commercials that had won prizes) than a selection of more 'ordinary' ads and their brands. With a first group of respondents, they tested for any possible effect immediately after the advertisements had been shown. With a second group, the test was carried out a week later, to see if the same effect would still be active. In both tests spontaneous and assisted recall were assessed, not only for the brand but also for certain 'executional' characteristics of the TV commercials. The results of both test groups showed that the respondents were indeed better able to remember the creative advertisements – both in terms of the brand shown and the characteristics displayed – than the run-of-the-mill ads. In other words, the research clearly demonstrated the recall effect of creative advertising and proved that this effect can extend over a longer period of time. It further demonstrated that creativity does not generate any additional recall effect when the respondents are assisted to remember the brand, in this instance by means of a list detailing the product categories of the brands they had seen in the commercials.

Till and Baack's third study investigated whether creative advertising can also have a positive influence on the purchasing intentions of consumers and on their overall attitude towards the advertising brands. Both elements – intention and attitude – were measured before and after the commercials were shown. However, the differences in the two sets of results were not significant. The researchers had two possible explanations. Firstly, they pointed out that in this test their selection of 'creative advertisements' had been made by a jury of professionals, whereas in the earlier tests the choice had been made by a group of students or respondents. Secondly, they suggested that it might be difficult to alter previously established brand attitudes and purchase intentions simply on the basis of a single viewing of an advertisement, no matter how creative it might be. Nevertheless, their general conclusion was that award-winning, creative advertising is more effective in terms of brand recall than less creative advertising.

Divergent or relevant?

Having said all this, the contention that creative advertising only distinguishes itself from other advertising by its ability to increase recall does not really go far enough. This, at least, is the opinion of US professors Yang and Smith (2009). They also carried out various research studies to establish how creative advertising actually works – and when. On the basis of their tests with

US consumers – the results of which were published in *Marketing Science* in 2009 – they argue that creative advertising works through processes of divergence and relevance, which can be applied to the brand, the product or even the advertisement itself.[5]

Divergence consists of five different dimensions:

1 *Originality*, which involves the advertisement being made with elements that are rare, surprising or deviate from the ordinary;

2 *Flexibility*, which means that the advertisement contains different ideas or changes of perspective;

3 *Elaboration*, which implies that the advertisement must contain unexpected details, or else is built up on the basis of simple ideas that can become ever more complex and sophisticated;

4 *Synthesis*, which requires the advertisement to bring together ideas and objects that would not normally be associated with each other;

5 *Artistic value*, which means that the advertisement must make use of artistic verbal impressions or attractive colours and shapes.[6]

In addition, a German study of 437 TV ad campaigns for 90 FMCG brands from January 2005 to October 2010 examined the relationships between consumers' perceptions of creativity and the sales figures for the products. They too determined creativity along the five dimensions of originality, flexibility, elaboration, synthesis and artistic value.

The findings were quite impressive. In general, the researchers concluded that a euro invested in a highly creative ad campaign had nearly double the sales impact of a euro spent on a non-creative campaign. They also discovered that, when used in combination, the creativity dimensions had widely varying effects. And that the most-used pairing – flexibility plus elaboration – as in fact one of the least effective. The most effective pairing – originality plus elaboration – had almost double the impact.[7]

Relevance finds its expression in elements that can be described as 'meaningful', 'appropriate' and 'valuable'. These elements can be brand-related (for example, new product information) or related to the advertising campaign itself (for example, meaningful music and images).

Yang and Smith take as their starting point the position that creative advertising is not *either* divergent *or* relevant, but that its success is dependent upon an effective combination of the two: divergence by relevance. The results of their research show that creative advertising – in other words, advertising that is both divergent and relevant – has two important effects: a cognitive effect and an affective (or emotional) effect. The cognitive effect is based on the ability of creative advertising to ensure that people view the source – the advert – with an open mind and a less defensive attitude. Creativity therefore encourages the consumer to offer less resistance to the advertisement's attempts to convince him or her, a process that is known as 'desire to postpone closure' or DPC. This open attitude also means that the consumer will be more inclined to watch the same advert or commercial again and also more inclined to buy the product or brand being advertised.

In addition to its impact on the cognitive process, creative advertising also stimulates positive feelings in the consumers who watch, read or hear it. It is well doumented that this type of 'affective' reaction can have a strong influence on the way people react to advertisements and the information they contain. Here, too, the Yang and Smith research posits a direct link between purchasing behaviour and the willingness to repeat-view creative ads.

Their research also examined the extent to which creative advertising has the same effects on people who are strongly predisposed towards or against advertising in general. In this instance, Yang and Smith concluded that in people who have a strong predisposition, both the cognitive and the affective processes are activated by creative advertising. In people with a weak disposition – perhaps not surprisingly – the cognitive effect is scarcely noticeable. Nevertheless, creative advertising is still capable of generating positive feelings amongst this group. Or to put it another way: creative advertising always results in an emotional response amongst both committed and non-committed consumers.

What makes an advertisement a viral success?

The best viral advertising films on the internet in 2012 were not only for major brands, like Samsung, Procter & Gamble and M&Ms, but also for non-profit organizations such as Invisible Children, with its indictment of the massacres carried out by rebel leader Joseph Kony in Central Africa. The top three films in the following list all exceeded the magic barrier of 100 million views.

Top 10 Viral Ad Campaigns in 2012 (based on number of views)

1 Invisible Children – Kony – 213,108,436

2 Red Bull – Stratos – 171,028,643

3 Rovia – Angry Birds Space – 109,634,050

4 Samsung – Galaxy S III – 71,868,864

5 Intel, Toshiba – The Beauty Inside – 55,171,199

6 M&Ms – Just My Shell – 48,371,667

7 P&G – Proud Sponsor of Moms 2012 – 46,966,905

8 TNT– Your Daily Dose of Drama – 43,780,141

9 Samsung – LeBron's Day – 42,298,532

10 Rovio – Angry Birds Star Wars – 41,422,263

These were all advertising films produced by professional makers on behalf of their advertising clients. The most important criterion for viral success is a captivating, memorable and creative concept. In most cases, a powerful musical accompaniment is another key factor. Irrespective of the length of the film, the intention is to first attract and then hold the attention of the viewer. If it wants to be seen and shared, an advertising film must generate strong emotions (either positive or negative), must include spectacular effects and – above all – must be 'cool'.

SOURCES Learmonth, M (2012) and Unruly (2012) Global Viral Video Ads

Figures from advertising expert John Hallward confirm that it is precisely the combination of divergence and relevance – he calls it 'difference' – which provides the persuasive power of an advertisement. When advertising focuses too heavily on originality and recall, there is a danger that the brand message will be lost. In addition to divergence and relevance, Hallward also cites the credibility of an ad or TV commercial as being another main contributory factor to its overall persuasiveness.

These findings not only underline the importance of emotions in advertising, but can also help advertisers and the makers of advertisements to better adjust their campaigns to reflect the expectations of their target groups. For example, with more committed consumers it may be beneficial to place the emphasis on the stimulation of their curiosity, using divergent elements that have a stronger effect on the cognitive process, such as the level of implementation and synthesis. Informative messages will work well in this context. For less committed consumers, it is probably better to use divergent elements that can activate their emotions, such as originality and artistic value (see Chapter 5).

FIGURE 3.1   The mechanisms of advertising concepts

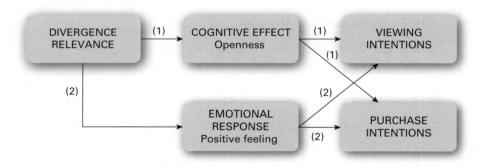

(1) Pathway is significant in cases of high commitment

(2) Pathway is significant in cases of both high and low commitment

Creative advertising is both divergent and relevant. It works in two distinct ways. On the one hand, creative advertising induces a cognitive effect in the target group, by helping people to adopt a less defensive attitude and to be more open towards the message and the brand. This openness is beneficial both for the viewing intentions and the purchase intentions of the target group. However, the cognitive effect is only activated in people who are already well-disposed towards advertising. On the other hand, creative advertising also evokes an emotional response, because it generates positive feelings, which are again beneficial for both viewing intentions and purchase intentions. This emotional effect is always active, and works irrespective of whether the target group is well-disposed towards advertising or not.

(Source: Yang and Smith, 2009)

Creativity rhymes with effectivity

The research carried out by Yang and Smith (2009) contends that, to a large extent, it is the emotional component in advertisments that is responsible for the success of an advertising campaign. This has been confirmed by a detailed study by the English advertising association, the IPA (with marketing specialist Peter Field), which since 2010 has been published together with the famous Gunn Report. Once again, the evidence shows that almost half (47 per cent) of the award-winning creative campaigns surveyed by the study made use of emotional means of communication, while this figure drops to just over a third (35 per cent) for non-winning campaigns.[8]

Creative campaigns for dummies

Creativity is subjective. For creative teams it will mean one thing, while for marketing scientists it may mean something completely different. Is there a magic formula for making creative advertisements? Are there general techniques or patterns that characterize such advertisements? Researchers Goldenberg, Mazursky and Solomon (1999)[9] from the University of Jerusalem have tried to provide answers to these crucial questions. From the results of their research they were able to distill 16 possible templates or creative techniques, divided between 6 different categories, which are frequently to be found in award-winning creative ads:

- ✚ *Pictorial analogy*: use symbols and metaphors, sometimes in an exaggerated fashion, to emphasize the value of the product;

- ✚ *Extreme situations*: use unrealistic scenarios to highlight the strengths of the product;

- ✚ *Consequence*: demonstrate in an exaggerated or unexpected manner the dire consequences that may result if the product is not purchased;

❖ *Competition*: underline the strengths of the product by allowing it to 'compete' with a product or event from another category;

❖ *Interactive experiment*: encourage the public to experience the benefits of the product on the basis of an interactive experiment with the medium itself;

❖ *Dimensionality alteration*: play with the different dimensions of a product in relationship to its environment, such as time and space.

(**SOURCE** Goldenberg, J, Mazursky, D and Solomon, S 1999)

However, the IPA research is even more significant for the manner in which it establishes the link between creativity and the effectiveness of advertising. It has done this by analysing the details of 435 campaigns conducted between 1994 and 2010. The results reveal that award-winning, creative campaigns are much more effective than the campaigns that miss out on the prizes. This is because of the larger 'excess share of voice' (ESOV) that the award winners are able to generate. ESOV is equivalent to 'share of voice' minus 'share of market'. When the results are assessed in relation to ESOV levels, the link between creativity and effectivity becomes even clearer, according to the IPA. During the 16 years of the study, award-winning campaigns were seven times more efficient in growing the market share of their brand than the ordinary campaigns. Moreover, there is also a discernable trend that suggests that creative campaigns become even more effective as time passes. The award-winning creative campaigns that took place during the second half of the study period were 12 times more effective than their prize-less rivals, whereas during the first half of the study period they were 'only' three times more effective.

Creative campaigns are also more cost-efficient. The data suggests that with the same ESOV level an award-winning creative campaign will generate twice as much growth in market share as a non-award winner. It is also worth noting that award-winning creative campaigns offer a better guarantee of effectiveness, which, according to the researchers, means that they are more reliable investments. For the same level of investment, the award winners provide a higher level of success, which goes beyond a straightforward increase in market share. In particular, their impact is greater in terms of both volume and value for the brand concerned. And as if this were not enough, the research further suggests that a campaign becomes even more effective the more often it is honoured with an award.

The same research points to yet another advantage of creative advertising, which can again be linked with effectivity and which is likely to become increasingly relevant in the digital, connected world in which we live. Moreover, it is an advantage that can be exploited outside the realms of the paid media. What is it? It is the 'buzz' effect. 'Buzz' or fame goes far beyond simple brand awareness. It relates to the extent to which people talk (both online and offline) about the advertising campaign, so that some consumers might even become ambassadors for the advertising brand (see Chapter 1). The IPA study compared the buzz and fame scores for creative award-winning and non-award-winning campaigns. It came to the conclusion that the proportion of award-winning campaigns that obtain a high buzz score has increased dramatically in recent years; from less than a third (28 per cent) in 2004 to an impressive 70 per cent at the time of writing. During the same period, the number of award-less campaigns with a high buzz score has risen from just 18 per cent to 29 per cent. This rise in the buzz scores of creative award-winning campaigns is one of the main reasons why the IPA contends that these campaigns are becoming even more effective as time goes by (see above and also Chapter 1).

Summary

The debate about the irritation caused by advertising continues to rage. Research has shown that both classic and digital media are facing this same problem. It is not the quantity of advertising that annoys people. It is the quality: too often, they just don't like it. Fortunately, research (backed by practice) has also shown that the public does appreciate creative advertising and is willing to share this advertising with others in their environment; for example, via social media. Put simply, the essence of good advertising is good *creative* advertising. Consumers only remember creative advertising; the rest they forget.

Creative advertising is therefore a much more effective way of setting and meeting brand objectives – a fact that is supported by extensive research carried out in the United Kingdom. To achieve this, creative advertising must be both divergent for and relevant to the consumer. Emotions also play a key role in creative advertisements. These ads and commercials, by virtue of the emotional response they evoke, always have an effect on consumers, whether they are committed or not.

Finally, creative advertising generates extra buzz and additional word-of-mouth advertising.

Practical inspiration

1 Evaluate your brand campaigns: is there a link between creativity and effectivity?

2 Is there consistency in your creative campaigns or do you use a different creative concept for each campaign? What are the advantages and disadvantages?

3 Evaluate recent campaigns for their relevance to the consumer and their divergent characteristics.

4 To what extent do your campaigns play on the emotions of consumers? Which emotions?

5 Do you look to achieve a high buzz score with your campaigns or is this just an added bonus if it happens?

CASE STUDY   Snickers: 'You're Not You When You're Hungry'

Snickers's 'You're Not You When You're Hungry' campaign is a perfect example of how creativity works. The campaign tapped into the insight that when you are hungry, you are not quite yourself. Some people turn into divas – represented in the ad by the actress Joan Collins. Some do strange things, like football player Rio Ferdinand, who started talking about sewing on Twitter. Others just became plain weird.

The creative ad was thus both relevant and divergent: on the one hand the nutty chocolate bar profiled itself as the hunger solution to 'sort you out'. On the other hand it did so in a surprisingly original way.

And that this was also effective, is proven by the fact that the campaign received not only a golden Global Effie in 2011, as well as a Creative Effectiveness Lion and a Silver Cyber Lion in 2012, but it also achieved its goals of driving up penetration (reaching 1.24 million more households than during the previous year), regaining its market value share (and even surpassing it by 2011) and re-establishing Snickers's fame as the world's best and biggest-selling chocolate bar (earning over 400 million incremental and unpaid media impressions).

SOURCE Effie Worldwide (2011). Snickers. You're not you when you're hungry. Consulted online: www.effie.org

Notes

1   Oxford Dictionaries [accessed 20 December 2013] *Oxford* [Online] http://oxforddictionaries.com

2   Hallward, J (2007) *Gimme! The human nature of successful marketing,* John Wiley & Sons, New Jersey

3   Pieters, R, Warlop, L and Wedel, M (2002) Breaking through the clutter: benefits of advertising originality and familiarity for brand attention and memory, *Management Science,* 48 (6), pp 765–81

4   Till, B D and Baack, D W (2005) Recall and persuasion: does creativity matter? *Journal of Advertising,* 34 (3), pp 47–57

5   Yang, X and Smith, R E (2009) Beyond attention effects: modeling the persuasive emotional effects of advertising creativity, *Marketing Science,* 28 (5), pp 935–49

6   Smith, R E, MacKenzie, S B, Yang, X, Buchholz, L M and Darley, W K (2007) Modeling the determinants and effects of creativity, *Marketing Science,* 26 (6), pp 819–33

7   Reinartz, R and Saffert, P (2013) Creativity in advertising: when it works and when it doesn't, *Harvard Business Review,* 91 (6), pp 107–12

8   IPA [accessed 20 November 2012] The Link Between Creativity and Effectiveness, *New/more findings from The Gunn Report and the IPA Databank, 2010/2011 update* [Online] http://thinkbox.tv/server/show/nav.1372

9   Goldenberg, J, Mazursky, D and Solomon, S (1999) The fundamental templates of quality ads, *Marketing Science* 18 (3), pp 333–51

04

Consumers as advertising creatives

The new spirit of the age, which favours the empowerment of both citizens and consumers, combined with the rapid rise of social media, has resulted in a world where individual consumers can give free rein to the development and sharing of their creative talents. They can even become a brand in their own right and can certainly help to make or break other commercial brands. Media attention is what they are seeking. But what is the real brand value of user-generated advertising in today's modern market and how can marketing and communications professionals succeed in transforming the consumers' creative inspiration and energy into a positive process? And are user-generated campaigns really more credible than classic campaigns?

What exactly is user-generated content (UGC)? The name says it all. It is content created by members of the public about the brands they use. In other words, it is free and not created by professionals. Moreover, it is content that is made available to a wider public by media such as the internet. Or up to a point – because not all UGC is freely available and accessible to everyone, since sometimes it will be reserved for the eyes and ears of a closed community.[1]

Originally, UGC was a true niche activity. Today, however, it is increasingly possible to talk – according to some – of a 'communication democracy', in which the internet is giving ever-larger amounts of power to users. Nowadays, everyone is free to throw their opinion about almost anything onto the net. UGC is the natural consequence of the growth of online communities and social networks.

One of the earliest forms of content generated by and for the public was the numerous blogs that appeared just after the turn of the millennium. Podcasts and forums have also now been with us for a number of years. You can read this in Wikipedia, the online encyclopedia, which is yet another form of content generated by non-professionals. But for many people YouTube, Facebook, Instagram and Twitter are now the most popular platforms for the publication, sharing and spreading of online content.

It was expected that by 2013 the number of people creating online content would have grown to 114.5 million.[2] 'Amateurs' will make 70 per cent of all content about brands on YouTube, Facebook and Twitter. Just 30 per cent will comprise output from marketing professionals.[3] On the other side of the coin however, the most shared films on the internet continue to be made by professional companies working for commercial advertisers of one kind or another (see Chapter 3).

In other words, nowadays the ball is well and truly in the court of the consumers. This finds its expression in the information and experiences they share and in the brand-related content they create. The classic example of brand-related content that was not generated by professionals (and one which set many of these professionals thinking!) dates back to 2006. This was the now-legendary Mentos/Diet Coke film, in which two amateurs in doctors' coats dropped a couple of Mentos mints into a bottle of Diet Coke, which resulted in a spectacular fountain of foam. This ad was viewed millions of times on YouTube and the sale of Mentos in the United States increased by 15 per cent. In addition, the amount of free PR was huge and the total value of the media attention was estimated at $100 million.[4]

Since then, almost every marketer had been asking the same question: are consumers perhaps better creators of advertising than the professionals? And if so, how on earth can they create a 'Mentos effect' for their brand?

Success factors for brands

In the meantime, a number of brands have already had some experience of involving their consumers in advertising campaigns.

In 2009, for example, Proximus, the Belgian mobile telephone operator, launched its 'Generation Movie Project', which called on young people via social media, TV and YouTube to take part in their television commercial. The result? The very first user-generated TV commercial in Belgium, a world record for the most participants in a televised ad and a viral hit with the younger public.

In The Netherlands McDonald's tried something similar: 114,000 consumers submitted their suggestions for a new type of burger, 744,000 Dutchmen and women voted for their favourite and the winning entry is now famed throughout the country. And it is much the same story with Doritos in the United States. Every year during the Super Bowl they use a very clever example of brand-related UGC. Their 'Crash the Super Bowl' campaign invites fans to create their own Doritos TV commercial, which has a chance of being broadcast live during the advertising breaks in the big game. In 2012 more than 6,000 consumers tried their luck at winning the mega-prize of $1 million.

Since its arrival on the scene, UGC has been a source of both interest and concern for the professional marketers. In many respects, UGC and its effect on brands is not yet fully understood. UGC campaigns are certainly popular, but are they effective? Do they offer a good return? In fact, is there not a possibility that the UGC generated by consumers might not sometimes work against the interests of the brands?

On the basis of empirical research carried out in 2012 by George Christodoulides (Henley Business School, University of Reading), Colin Jevons (Monash University) and Jennifer Bonhomme (Digital Planning Consultant), a model has been created which offers new insights into the link between the drivers for UGC and the involvement of the consumer (the extent to which the brand is experienced as personally relevant and important) and its effect on brand equity (which is generally determined by awareness, loyalty, associations, attributes and qualities).[5]

The researchers have identified four drivers that can act as motivation for the generation of UGC: co-creation, empowerment, community and self-concept. Their hypothesis contends that the more strongly these four drivers are present, the more strongly the consumer will feel involved with a brand:

❖ *Co-creation* relates to all situations where consumers collaborate with a company or with other consumers to make something, such as online content or even a product. The growing number of online conversations about brands and products shows that the consumer is certainly interested in this kind of collaboration and dialogue. Through this process of co-creation consumers regard themselves as a valuable and integral part of the company or brand. No longer satisfied with the range of experiences provided for them by this company or brand, they now want to create their own experiences.

❖ *Empowerment* is connected to the fact that many consumers no longer want to be influenced by marketing and advertising, preferring instead to take control of the decision-making process. In a reversal of roles, they use the internet and their own content as weapons to put pressure on the marketers and advertisers to take account of their wishes.

As a result of the development of social media, numerous digital communities have come into being. Communities are groups of people linked together by a common activity or a common characteristic. Today, the members of many communities are connected by their interest in a particular brand, using the internet as their central medium. The majority of the members of these communities is no longer prepared to consume in a passive manner, but want to interact, share experiences and co-create. People who are closely involved in this type of brand community are usually more emotionally committed to the brand in question. They identify more closely than others with this brand and are loyal to it.

❖ *Community* is the third driver for brand-related UGC. UGC offers consumers the possibility to express themselves through sharing ideas and experiences with the other community members.

❖ *Self-concept* As long ago as 1955, a study demonstrated that brands can be vehicles for self-expression.[6] Consumers try to express themselves and distinguish themselves from others by the choice of brands they make. Social psychologists describe self-concept as the perception of the own self. It is a collection of a person's self-evaluations about who they are and how they function. Self-concept seeks to build a bridge between the imperfect 'me' of the present and the perfect 'me' of the future. This is achieved through a process of self-appreciation, self-development, self-identification and peer recognition.[7] The social dimension of UGC offers a platform for this process.

What conclusions can be drawn from this quantitative research? Three of the four drivers – co-creation, community and self-concept – have a positive impact on the involvement of the consumer with the brand. Moreover, this involvement in turn has a positive impact on brand perception and brand equity. However, the contention that there is also a correlation between the empowerment driver and involvement is not proven by the data. Empowerment has no significant impact on brand involvement. In fact, it is often claimed (as already mentioned above) that empowerment is based on the dislike that many consumers feel for what they regard as marketing manipulation and their desire to no longer be influenced. Or could it be that consumers who participate in UGC – which was everyone in the case of this study – are already more empowered of their own accord?

An opposing hypothesis was also investigated; namely, the existence or non-existence of the so-called 'feedback loop'. Can the value of a brand alone influence the consumer's perception of co-creation, empowerment, community and self-concept? Or to express it differently: is it possible that the more value a consumer attaches to a brand, the more likely he or she will be to think that the brand is based on co-creation, empowerment, community and self-concept? This reverse hypothesis – that value of brand can have a positive impact on the four UGC drivers – was partly confirmed. Brand value does indeed have an impact on three of the four drivers: co-creation, empowerment and community. But the concept that more brand value leads to more self-concept (self-expression, self-cultivation, self-development, identification) was not proven. The authors have an explanation (so far unsupported) for this apparent anomaly: consumers who are driven by self-concept, they argue, will be more likely to create UGC for less well-known brands, because these will allow them to be freer and more creative, thereby allowing them in turn to exercise more influence on the perceptions of other consumers.

Be that as it may, it is certainly the case that a brand with strong brand equity has a better chance of developing a successful UGC campaign, thanks to the strong influence of the co-creation, empowerment and community drivers.

Personality makes the difference

The research by Christodoulides, Jevons and Bonhomme (2012) was in the first instance focused on active UGC participants. It showed how involvement in brand-related UGC can help to change the perception and value of the brand in question in a positive manner.

However, another study carried out by Forrester Research, covering no fewer than 57,924 North American (Canada and the United States) and 16,473 European UGC users, shows that only a quarter of consumers are seriously active on social media platforms. These active users – the people who actually create content and place it online – amount to just 24 per cent of the US respondents and 23 per cent of their European counterparts. The users who assess and comment on website content represented 36 per cent and 33 per cent of their respective survey populations.[8]

In this context, the Nielsen Research Bureau applies the rough 1/10/90 rule. One per cent of social media users make content, 10 per cent share and give comment on content, but the largest group – the remaining 90 per cent – simply 'consumes' that content passively. In this respect, the 1/10/90 rule endorses the 2-step-flow model of advertising (as discussed in Chapter 1).

For this reason, it is vital for the success of digital participative campaigns to identify the right target group. Almost intuitively, many marketers think that this means the early adopters. However, there is no evidence to show that early adopters will take on the role of pioneers, actively stimulating the larger, passive group of users to participation.[9] It requires more than straightforward demographic segmentation to determine the profile of the active UGC consumer. Criteria such as age and gender alone are insufficient. For example, psychological differences between consumers also help to influence whether or not someone will actively create UGC.

In September 2012, the Singaporean researcher Dominic Yeo (Hong Kong Baptist University) published the results of his research into the psychological profiles of digital consumers, with the aim of identifying the best target groups for interactive campaigns.[10] Combining an extensive literature study with a survey of 656 YouTube users, Yeo concluded that participation in social media was determined either by the 'own self' (individualistic) or by 'the others' (relational). The starting point for the research was the so-called 'Big Five': the five universal personality traits possessed by people. These traits offer a framework in which the individual characteristics of consumers can be bundled. The five traits in question are:

1 *Extraversion*: the tendency to be social, communicative and self-confident; someone who enjoys change and excitement;

2 *Agreeableness*: the tendency to trust others; someone who empathizes and cooperates;

3 *Conscientiousness*: the tendency to behave in a socially responsible manner; someone who is dedicated, with a feeling for organization and an ability to adjust;

4 *Neuroticism*: the tendency to display chronically negative emotions; someone who expresses these emotions in their behaviour;

5 *Openness to experience*: the tendency to be intellectually curious and artistically inclined; someone who is prepared to consider alternatives.

According to Yeo, the extent to which these different personality traits are present in a person will determine the type of media they prefer and their manner of using it. The research shows clearly that there is a correlation between the personal characteristics of a consumer and his or her preference for a particular media. For example, Yeo's survey of YouTube users revealed that the 'extraversion' trait is frequently to be found in people who have a preference for humoristic films; the more neurotic users are generally more inclined to opt for drama and informative films.

On the basis of the 'Big Five' and the insights into media use that they reveal, Yeo distinguishes between two basic types of consumer. On the one hand, there are the utilitarian, instrumental consumers, who are rational and practical by nature. On the other hand, there are the hedonic, emotional consumers, who are more focused on experiences and pleasure. In terms of media use, the instrumental consumers have a preference for platforms that they find useful or informative, while their emotional counterparts like platforms that give them enjoyment.

Naturally, the level of involvement with media – the extent to which a medium is regarded by the consumer as being more or less relevant – is also a key determining factor in media use. Involvement influences the cognitive aspect of consumer behaviour, such as actively searching for information, giving and seeking attention, being convinced, etc. But involvement does not necessarily need to be cognitive. For example, it has been shown that involvement in the internet has both cognitive and affective dimensions.

Consumers are typified on the basis of two dynamics that determine the extent and the nature of their online participation. The two consumer profiles – the instrumental and the emotional – correlate with these two forms of participation:

> **Individualist participation** is determined by the 'own self', is more hedonic and situation-dependent. Individualist users are emotional consumers who are looking first and foremost for pleasure, who are emotionally involved to a certain degree, who prefer light-hearted videos and who participate in a passive way. They search for films and watch them, but do little more than that.

> **Relational participation** is more dependent upon the personality of the consumer him- or herself. The relational user is more task-oriented, is cognitively involved with the film and is motivated to learn more by engaging with other users. For this reason, relational users tend to opt for more informative films and their response to these films is much more participative. For example, they will give ratings to the videos and write comments.

What do all these conclusions mean for an online campaign in concrete terms? The first wave of the campaign should be targeted at the interactive, relational users (also known as the instrumental consumers), since this is the group who can be most easily motivated to participate and whose participation will be most active. These relational users are also easier to identify than the individualists. Relational users are characterized above all by the personality traits of extraversion and neuroticism.

The compulsive behaviour of online consumers was also the subject of an internal paper by BBDO (2011): *Seducing the Social Super Ego*. This paper argued that 'digital natives' regard social media as an extension of real life. For them, it is the most natural way to express themselves and to give themselves a place in society. This has a strong narcissistic element: their online profile reflects their ideal image; every aspect of their life must be shared and completely 'up-to-date'; their popularity is measured on the basis of 'likes' and online comments, etc.[11]

A recent study that appeared in the *Journal of Brand Management* examined the relationship between so-called 'self-expressive' brands that are 'Liked' on Facebook, and consumers' brand advocacy in online and offline settings. A survey of 265 Facebook users revealed as well that consumers 'Like' brands that express their inner and social selves. Self-expressive brands reflecting their inner or social self encourage consumers to offer positive word of mouth on social networks. Further, self-expressive brands on Facebook positively influence consumers' brand acceptance, and their willingness to forgive their 'Liked' brands for wrongdoing.[12]

In relation to UGC, yet another study confirmed that 'ego-defensive' and social functions of attitude are the most explanatory power for users to want to create content and thus for the success of UGC campaigns. The ego-defensive function compels people to protect themselves from personal insecurity and threats coming from others. UGC campaigns help these people to minimize personal doubts and feel part of a community. The social function, logically, has to do with peer pressure and interaction with friends. So yet another reason why UGC campaigns are popular: they help people to connect and make them feel important.[13]

So, if the first wave of a campaign is aimed at the relational users, the second wave should seek to include the less active, individualist users as well. However, the individualists are less easy to track down and reach on the basis of their 'Big Five' characteristics, although Yeo does show that such users, more than their relational counterparts, typically opt for lighter content with a higher entertainment level. Similarly, individualist users will be attracted by the more hedonic aspects of products, rather than by products with a higher instrumental value.

FIGURE 4.1   Advertising message per UGC campaign wave

	1st wave	2nd wave
RELATIONAL PARTICIPATION	Instrumental informative communication	
INDIVIDUALIST PARTICIPATION		Pleasure, entertainment emotional communication

> With regard to user-generated content, consumers are stimulated to relational
> or individual participation online. In the first wave, instrumental and informative
> messages are important. In the second wave, the emphasis can be placed more
> squarely on emotional communication.
>
> (Source: Yeo, 2012)

Consequently, the second wave of the campaign should focus more on the emotional stimuli of the brand, so that the individualist users (the emotional consumers) can also be attracted and motivated to produce UGC. Offering incentives in exchange for participation can often help to push them in the right direction.

However, it is important to note that individualist and relational participation are not mutually exclusive; one does not necessarily rule out the other. In reality, communication is a continual dialogue between individualist and relational aspects, between affect and cognition, between the emotional and the instrumental. Similarly on social media, consumers select products, services or experiences on the basis of both individual and relational considerations.

Finally, another research study that appeared in the *Journal of Advertising Research* came to the same conclusions as Yeo when it comes to e-mailings and thus so-called electronic word of mouth (eWOM). As a first, not quite surprising, conclusion, the researchers stated that recipients who receive e-mails from close interpersonal sources are more willing to forward them than if they were coming from unfamiliar or commercial sources. Secondly, and more interestingly, those who receive more utilitarian or hedonic e-mails are more willing to forward them. And, third, those recipients who score high on the personality traits of extraversion and openness and low on conscientiousness, are more willing to forward a commercial e-mailing to others.[14]

Co-creation with stakeholders

UGC for advertising purposes cannot be viewed in isolation from the fundamental trend towards brand co-creation. Co-creation not only involves consumers, but can also be extended to other stakeholders. In this manner, co-creation becomes a process for the collective development of the value of a brand by all the different parties involved with the brand. This, at least, is the argument put forward by Professor Emerita Mary Jo Hatch (University of Virginia) and Professor Majken Schultz (Copenhagen Business School).[15]

According to Hatch and Schultz, various studies have already shown how co-creation is finding resonance with an increasing number of researchers, who believe that a brand (and its equity) are determined by the engagement of all its stakeholders. In other words, all the stakeholders are equally important as co-creators. However, until recently, the only stakeholder group to have been examined in any detail was the consumers.

Hatch and Schultz speak of co-creation as a new brand paradigm. According to them, the value that a brand represents is not simply 'manufactured' in a factory, but is the combined result of the co-creation of different network relationships and numerous social interactions, which take place within the wider context of the brand (and not exclusively in the marketing department or amongst the consumers). The greater the number of different access routes into the company and its resources, the greater the transparency for and the involvement of the stakeholders becomes. This means that all the relevant departments of a company (marketing, HR, sales and even the CEO) are effectively partners within the same co-creation process. Of course, there are certain risks attached to this process. There is a risk that the company will suffer damage to its reputation or lose control over its markets and activities. There is also a risk that the company will continue to listen too much to its own marketers and not enough to the consumers and the other stakeholders. But in return for accepting these risks, co-creation offers huge potential rewards, such as a better understanding of what customers and prospects really want.

The importance of involving all stakeholders has been confirmed by data research into digital communities carried out by Albert Muniz Jr (DePaul University) and Thomas O'Guinn (University of Illinois). They emphasize the partial view of the world that typifies the members of such communities, but also stress the traditions and rituals they embody. Likewise, they point to the sense of moral responsibility that the stakeholder groups bring to the dialogue with the company behind the brand.[16]

Another important function of these communities is the spreading of information, which enhances the transparency around the company and the brand. The social structure that the communities offer for the relationship between brand marketing and the consumer can often take the form of a network or even a central hub. In this manner, the brand's relation with the communities becomes a strategic responsibility; a responsibility that not only rests on the marketing function, but affects every member of the company. And because every function has its own stakeholders, this will lead to a complete stakeholder programme – although it remains open to question who should coordinate and lead this integrated approach and what its effect will be on the internal operations of the company.

Summary

In the first instance, UGC is driven by the consumers themselves, although companies are well advised to do what they can to stimulate the process. It has been shown conclusively that involvement in UGC has a positive effect on brand value and brand equity.

The most important points in this respect are: identifying the right target group; shaping the perception of consumers through co-creation; the development of a community around the brand; and connecting with the consumer's need for self-concept. This approach can also be extended to other stakeholders.

Using such an approach, it is possible to develop a deep relationship between the brand and the consumer, but also between the brand and the company. To avoid negative responses, brands should take proactive steps to involve consumers in their advertising campaigns.

Practical inspiration

1 What can you learn from content that consumers put online about your brand?

2 What are your own experiences with setting up your own campaigns in which consumers were allowed to play an active role?

3 Does your brand have a strategy for stimulating user-generated content?

4 Does your brand involve stakeholders other than consumers in its user-generated content campaigns?

5 How do you assess the advantages and disadvantages of user-generated content for your brand?

CASE STUDY　Lay's – 'Do Us A Flavor'

Lay's 'Do Us A Flavor' campaigns all over the world are cases in point that brands that integrate their customers – 'partner' with them – win as they both build a strong relationship with loyal, heavy buyers and reach a vast audience of light buyers. Since 2008, Lay's has challenged consumers across the world to help create the next best-selling chip flavour as a limited edition. This creative crowdsourcing has generated more than 8 million consumer submissions worldwide and led to a significant increase in global sales. Just as importantly, it enhanced the consumers' sense of ownership of the brand. The recent US campaign – to celebrate Lay's 75th birthday in 2013 – broke all previous records: 3.8 million flavours were submitted in just 12 weeks. The campaign generated 955 million story impressions and 1.26 billion PR impressions, resulting in weekly sales increase of 12 per cent. The campaigns have been rewarded several times, among which Effies, in several countries.

SOURCES

Pepsico (2011) Lay's Netherlands 'Do Us a Flavour' campaign wins Dutch Effie. Consulted online: www.pepsico.com

Champagne, C (2013) How Lay's got its chips to taste like chicken and waffles. Consulted online: www.fastcocreate.com

Chang, G (2013) Do Lay's a favor, submit a flavor. Consulted online: www.digitallabblog.com

Notes

1   Christodoulides, G, Jevons, C and Bonhomme, J (2012) Memo to marketers: quantitative evidence for change. How user-generated content really affects brands, *Journal of Advertising Research*, **52** (1), pp 53–64

2   eMarketer [accessed 26 March 2012] User generated content: more popular than profitable, *eMarketer Digital Intelligence* [Online] http://www.emarketer.com/Report.aspx?emarketer_2000549

3   360i (2009) *The State of Search*, A 360i Working Paper

4   Creamer, M [accessed 27 April 2011] Ad age agency of the year: the consumer, *Advertising Age* [Online] http://adage.com/article/news/ad-age-agency-year-consumer/114132/

5   See 1

6   Gardner, B and Levy, S (1955) The product and the brand, *Harvard Business Review*, **33** (2), pp 33–39

7   Verschueren, K and Gadeyne, E (2007) *Handboek diagnostiek in de leerlingenbegeleiding*, Garant: Antwerp.

8   Forrester Research [accessed online 24 April 2012] North American Technographics Online Benchmark Survey, Q3 2011 and European Technographics Online Benchmark Survey, Q3 2011, *Forrester Research* [Online] http://www.forrester.com/North+American+Technographics+Online +Benchmark+Survey+Q3+2011+US+Canada/-/E-SUS843 and http://www.forrester.com/European+Technographics+Online+Benchmark +Survey+Q3+2011/-/E-SUS838

9   Nielsen [accessed 14 April 2012] Participation Inequality: Encouraging More Users to Contribute, *Nielsen Norman group* [Online] http://www.nngroup.com/articles/participation-inequality/

10   Yeo, D T E (2012) Social-media early adopters don't count. How to seed participation in interactive campaigns by psychological profiling of digital consumers, *Journal of Advertising Research*, **52** (3), pp 297–308

11   Blackman, S J and Choquelle, P -J *et al* [accessed 17 April 2012] *Seducing the social super ego. Proximity BBDO* [Online] http://www.scribd.com/doc/51400682/Social-Super-Ego

12   Wallace, E, Buil, I and de Chernatony, L (2012) Facebook 'friendship' and brand advocacy, *Journal of Brand Management*, **20** (2), pp 128–46

13   Daugherty, T, Eastin, M S and Bright, L (2008) Exploring consumer motivations for creating user-generated content, *Journal of Interactive Advertising*, **8** (2), pp 16–25

14 Chiu, H-C *et al* (2007) The determinants of email receivers' disseminating behaviors on the internet, *Journal of Advertising Research*, December 2007, pp 524–34

15 Hatch, M J and Schultz, M (2010) Toward a theory of brand co-creation with implications for brand governance, *Journal of Brand Management*, **17** (8), pp 590–604

16 Muniz Jr, A M and O'Guinn, T C (2001) Brand community, *Journal of Consumer Research*, **27** (4), pp 412–32

✦ PART TWO ✦
Hybrid marketing

05

USP or ESP?

Another topic that is still the subject of much current debate is whether or not brands should use a rational claim (USP) or an emotional claim (ESP) for the marketing and communication of products and services. What are the advantages and disadvantages of both these advertising strategies and does it make a difference if the brand in question has a high level of brand equity or is relatively unknown in the market? Which of the two strategies do market leaders follow? And do brands really need to make a choice at all?

What is the purpose of advertising? The late Professor Andrew Ehrenberg (founder of the Ehrenberg-Bass Institute of Marketing Science in Australia) summarized his views on this matter in the year 2000: its purpose is to link a certain image or a certain added value to a brand, so that the brand can distinguish itself from its competitors in the minds of consumers.[1] And, indeed, marketing communication is to a large extent a question of 'making the difference'. The socio-economic context of brands may change, but the core of the matter is still the same as it has always been: making clear to consumers precisely what it is that sets a brand apart from its rivals.

How to make a difference

The insight that a product needs to offer a 'unique selling proposition' (USP), which the competition finds it difficult to claim or reproduce, was first put forward as early as 1961, when the US advertiser Rosser Reeves developed the USP approach for advertising purposes. Since then, the effective communication of a product's USP has been regarded as an essential element in any successful advertising campaign. Initially, it was believed – and strongly believed – that consumers would be capable of making rational purchasing decisions if they were offered an easy-to-view range and sufficient time to make the choice. However, as the years passed, the number of products and services – and their copies – has grown exponentially. This put the ability of brands to distinguish themselves under increasing pressure, particularly in mature markets.

Moreover, many people in marketing circles were gradually coming to the conclusion that human beings were perhaps too emotional to make purely rational choices. They argued that products are often seen as 'different' by the public precisely because they offer a human and emotional added value. People like to feel that they belong; this is a natural and universal impulse.[2] For this reason, they like to identify with a brand, to interact with it and perhaps even become an ambassador for it, sometimes without ever having actually bought the product or service in question (although examples of this kind of brand loyalty tend to be found at the luxury end of the market, such as Ferrari cars).[3] This phenomenon – the power of the consumer's emotional bond with a product – is known as the emotional selling proposition (ESP). These are the emotional stimuli that can persuade a prospect to make a purchase.

A 1989 study by Burke and Edell indicated three types of feelings that can be inspired by advertising:

❖ *Warm feelings* (affection, emotion, sentiment, etc);

❖ *Upbeat feelings* (happiness, action, energy, etc);

❖ *Negative feelings* (sadness, disgust, loneliness, etc).[4]

These types of feelings each translate into a different kind of marketing strategy or message: informative, positive emotional and negative emotional. And according to the academic researchers Patrick De Pelsmacker (University of Antwerp and University of Ghent) and Nathalie Dens (University of Antwerp), it is possible to contend that more rational, informative messages work less well than messages that play on people's emotions. Emotions, they argue, make it easier for people to remember things.[5] But is this true for all types of brands and all types of advertising?

In a recent comparative study De Pelsmacker and Dens (2010) tried to establish whether there was a correlation between new product strategies (for both new brands and extensions of existing brands) on the one hand and advertising strategies (informative and emotional) on the other. The aim was to see what effect, if any, this correlation might have on brand awareness and brand recall.[6] The three types of feelings and their associated strategies were investigated using a representative sample of Flemish consumers with different levels of involvement (high and low) and two different products (laptop computers and chocolate bars) in two different categories. The results of the research confirmed that the extension of an existing, well-known product is better received by the public than the message of an entirely new, still unknown product. The 'fame' of the mother brand has a positive influence on the extension. Because it is logical that a known brand name is easier to remember than an unknown one, it is possible to conclude – supported in part by the empirical evidence provided by De Pelsmacker and Dens – that consumers will more easily remember the extensions of existing brands than totally new ones. What is more, an extension of a well-known brand scores well for both awareness and recall, irrespective of the type of advertising used, whereas with new and unknown brands, the type of advertising and the message it projects can make a huge difference.

In other words, the research conducted by De Pelsmacker and Dens shows that the choice of advertising message is dependent upon the subject of the communication (a new brand or a brand extension) and on the objective, and that this choice will either have a greater or lesser effect depending on the type of product or brand. Bearing this in mind, one of the biggest challenges for the marketing of extensions is to convince consumers that the product is a derivative of the existing brand, rather than the brand itself. For unknown brands, the key test is to fix the brand in the memory of consumers, so that they will become familiar with it and recall it.

USPs work for known brands

If consumers are familiar with a brand and have a reasonable level of knowledge about it, the researchers claim that they will use its advertising to seek confirmation of what they already know rather than seeking for new information. This means that when a consumer is extremely knowledgeable about a brand, it is only necessary to communicate minimal (or no) product information. Using this same reasoning, unknown brands need to provide consumers with more details about the characteristics of their products and services, since only then will they be able to evaluate these products and services properly. Or is it actually the other way around? De Pelsmacker and Dens have investigated and tested the different hypotheses.

As previously mentioned, advertising strategies can be divided into two broad categories. On the one hand there is informational advertising, which informs consumers about one or more benefits of the brand. It is self-evident that USPs are ideal for use in this kind of advertising. Logically, informative messages also require the consumers to process more information than emotional messages. The risk with these kinds of informational messages is that the consumers are not willing or able to process all this new information. And it is equally logical that the more information that is packed into an advertisement, the less likely it is that the consumer will be able to remember all of it. For this reason, a tendency has developed to try to reach the consumer with different (but complementary) messages via different channels ('unity in diversity').

Naturally enough, emotional messages seek to arouse the emotions of consumers. In the past, various research studies have shown that the levels of brand recall are much higher with emotional advertising messages than informative ones.[7] Moreover, positive emotions act as an aid to memory, so that brand names 'stick' more easily in the consumer's mind.[8] On the basis of this reasoning, new brands can gain maximum benefit by seeking to communicate positive emotional messages. And the reverse is also true: in the case of negative emotional messages, the consumer is more likely to focus on the content and delivery of the message than on the brand itself: the brain needs to process more impulses, so that there is less room for processing – and remembering – the brand. This means that new brands in particular will suffer from negative emotional messages, since the processing of the new name alone already requires more mental effort than the names of known brands. So the moral is clear: new brands need to work with positive emotional messages.

'Known brands reap the biggest rewards from informative messages'

The research carried out by De Pelsmacker and Dens concludes – perhaps surprisingly but nonetheless logically – that known brands reap the biggest rewards from informative messages with USPs. Informative messages that contain new product information are therefore the best strategy for existing brands, because the consumer is already familiar with the brand and consequently has more room for the processing of other information about the new product. This is even more true for the extensions of existing brands. The only condition is that the new characteristics (USPs) of the extension are explained clearly and in detail in the informative message. Only then will the consumer be able to register the novelty of the extension in relation to what he or she already knows about the brand.

In view of the fact that emotional messages are better suited to creating or strengthening brand image, the researchers assume that this type of message stimulates very little processing of product information. Just as USPs are more appropriate for informative messages, so ESPs work better for emotional messages. Likewise, just as USPs work better for the extensions of known brands, so ESPs are more appropriate for new (and as yet) unknown brands. The re-launching of the Apple brand around the turn of the century is a good example of this phenomenon. By the middle of the 1990s Apple had almost reached the end of the road. To re-focus the attention of consumers on the Apple brand, in 1997 CEO Steve Jobs commissioned the highly emotional 'Think Different' campaign. This campaign succeeded brilliantly in making the brand known — and loved – again. But for the more recent iPhone and iPad campaigns the company opted for a highly informational approach, with an emphasis on the USPs of the new products.

Having said all this, there is an increasing tendency for advertisers to try to get the best of both worlds. For example, the clothing retailer H&M repeatedly makes advertisements that combine a mix of emotional messages (glamorous models in hip clothes) and informative details (prices are always mentioned).

Emotions sell

If emotions determine our behaviour, how do they influence that behaviour when it comes to brands and the purchase of products? It was Gordon in 2006 who first argued that people do not receive information about brands passively, but transform that information into something that is personally relevant to them.[9]

Until recently, however, there was no real research to tell us about the effectiveness of this type of emotional branding and its effect on consumer behaviour. This gap in our knowledge has now been filled by a large-scale study carried out by John Rossiter (University of Wollongong) and Steve Bellman (Interactive Television Research Institute and Murdoch University). In an online survey they investigated the emotions of a representative sample of consumers in the United States. These were all purchasers of everyday products (petrol, washing powder, instant coffee and beer). The purpose was to establish how effective the use of emotions could be both in terms of influencing behaviour and increasing sales.[10] The researchers concluded that for products of this kind it was only possible to establish an emotional bond with the brand in roughly 25 per cent of cases, but that this 25 per cent was strongly attached to that brand and consequently rewarded the marketer with much higher sales and use of their products. In other words, emotionally attached consumers are the most profitable consumers, particularly if one bears in mind that the research also showed that these customers require no price incentives to remain loyal to the brand.

Moreover, this type of emotional branding seems to work just as effectively with men as with women. The perception that women are more open and react better to emotional messages is therefore not true – at least as far as this study is concerned. It is possible that emotional branding is even more effective in cases of high involvement, but this was not examined by Rossiter and Bellman. It was, however, something that De Pelsmacker and Dens looked at. They concluded that the extent to which a person is committed during the processing of a message is a key determining factor. Committed or involved consumers will better remember the brand and the USP in an informative message than in an emotional message. Why? Because informative messages require more cognitive processing and highly committed consumers are more prepared to make the necessary effort – which has a beneficial effect in terms of recall. In short, informational messages are very useful and very effective when the consumer is closely involved and (as mentioned earlier) familiar with the brand.

The opposite can be assumed for consumers with a low level of involvement, although this was not confirmed by the Flemish study. It is likely that the novelty of the new product is not sufficient to persuade them to undertake the necessary cognitive processing. Non-involved consumers lose attention more quickly, which means that the brand and/or its USP fail to stick in their memory for any length of time. They will be better able to remember the brand if they are targeted with an emotional message (see Chapter 3).

The research carried out by the British IPA database into the most effective advertising campaigns also concluded that campaigns with an emotional message are generally the most successful, followed by combined USP/ESP campaigns. Campaigns with a rational message were clearly the least effective of the three.[11]

Summary

Informative messages are recommended in cases of brand extension, because they focus in more detail on the new elements of the product and the advantages they can offer. Logically, USPs are best communicated with this type of informational message. An informative message contains more information about the product, so that the consumers will more easily understand the USP.

With new brands, consumers are more curious about the values for which the brand stands. Positive emotional messages can help to satisfy this curiosity, because they not only arouse interest but also stimulate recall, thanks to the warmth and happiness of the feelings they project. The best type of message to use is also dependent upon the level of involvement of the consumer. Informative messages are better for people with levels of high involvement, whereas the less committed respond better to emotional messages.

Practical inspiration

1 Evaluate the use of USPs and ESPs for your brand. Look for the connection with brand awareness and the involvement of your consumers.

2 Which strategy would be best for you if you want to bring a totally new product to the market?

3 Make an analysis of the use of USPs and ESPs in the campaigns of the top three brands in your sector.

4 Can you show a connection between the emotional factor in an advertising campaign and the commercial success of that campaign?

5 Can USPs and ESPs be used together in a campaign? Within the same concept or via different channels?

CASE STUDY   Febreze: 'Breathe Happy'

Febreze needed to convince consumers that it was genuinely superior to the competition in order to sustain its sales at a premium. Rather than simply selling its odour-eliminating power the rational way, Febreze let consumers experience it for themselves through real-life experiments. The brand's campaign line became 'Breathe Happy', combining the tangible aspects of its air care (its USP) with an emotionally uplifting message of happiness (thus, its ESP). Apart from winning a golden Euro Effie and a bronze Cannes Lion in 2012, as well as a Silver AME Award and a Silver North American Effie in 2013, its value share increased 19 per cent and an estimated 250 million people were reached.

SOURCE Effie Worldwide (2012). Febreze. Breathe happy global campaign. Consulted online: www.effie.org

Notes

1   Ehrenberg, A S C (2000) Repetitive advertising and the consumer, *Journal of Advertising Research*, **40** (6), pp 39–48

2   Rommen, K (2011) Developing relationships. Consumers as a source for sustainable competitive advantage, *Slideshare* [Online] http://slideshare.net/kevinrommen/developing-relationships-consumers-as-a-source-for-sustainable-competitive-advantage

3   Veloutsou, C (2009) Brands as relationship facilitators in consumer markets, *Marketing Theory*, **9** (1), pp 127–30

4   Burke, M C and Edell, J A (1989) The impact of feeling on ad-based affect and cognition, *Journal of Marketing Research*, **26** (1), pp 69–83

5   De Pelsmacker, P and Dens, N (2010) How advertising strategy affects brand and USP recall for new brands and extensions, *International Journal of Advertising*, **29** (2), pp 165–94

6   See 5

7   See 5

8   Geuens, M and De Pelsmacker P (1998) Feelings evoked by warm, erotic, humorous or non-emotional print advertising for alcoholic beverages, *Academy of Marketing Science Review*, **1**, pp 1–32

9   Gordon, W (2006) What do consumers do emotionally with advertising? *Journal of Advertising Research*, **46** (1), pp 2–10

10 Rossiter, J and Bellman, S (2012) Emotional branding pays off: how brands meet share of requirements through bonding, companionship and love, *Journal of Advertising Research*, **52** (3), pp 291–96

11 Pringle, H and Field, P (2008) *Brand Immortality: How brands can live long and prosper*, Kogan Page, London

06

Global or local?

In light of the increasing globalization of the world economy, there is a strong trend towards global brands, with marketing and advertising campaigns to match. But is such a globalized marketing strategy possible for every company and brand? Are we all destined to become global consumers, who only buy big and powerful global brands? Or are we going to fall back on our own local products?

The idea is that global campaigns must also lead to significant cost-efficiency savings. On the other side of the coin, many companies have begun to notice that consumers, particularly in Western countries, continue to be loyal to their local, regional products and also to their local, regional retailers, who are closer to them and have a better understanding of their needs. In response to this, a third trend has developed, in which global brands place a heavy emphasis on local concerns in their marketing and advertising campaigns: the so-called 'glocal' marketing.

Standardization vs adaptation

Since the 1960s, arguments have been raging about the advantages and disadvantages of standardization in advertising. Supporters say that standardized advertising campaigns for different international markets help to strengthen the worldwide strategy and global image of the brand. In a standardized strategy the starting point is that if the world is globalized, then there must also be such a thing as a globalized consumer culture. In this globalized world, consumers come into contact with the same products and brands, and they increasingly develop the same preferences. Viewed from this perspective, companies obtain their competitive advantage from the possibility of offering goods of a high quality at a low price; more specifically, a standard product or a good idea that is launched via standardized marketing campaigns in various markets. Examples of companies that are aware of and consciously choose this kind of global strategy are Apple, Gillette and Ikea.

Opponents of standardization (or rather, supporters of adaptation) claim that the interpretation of an advertising message is dependent upon cultural, historical, religious, linguistic, economic and social factors, so that it is not possible for companies simply to 'translate' the same advertising campaign into all the world's different markets. This explains why the world leader in the beer market – AB Inbev – deliberately adopts a strategy built around local brands. And contrary to what many people might think, even a company like AB Inbev's leading rival, Heineken, generates only 15 per cent of its turnover from its Heineken master brand, based on a global marketing campaign. The remaining 85 per cent is generated by numerous local brands with local advertising.

As mentioned above, there is also a third trend, which sees 'global' brands seeking to inject a strong 'local' element into their communication planning. This is what Nike has attempted to do with its sponsoring of various national football teams around the world. Procter & Gamble also uses a similar two-pronged strategy, with strong world brands that are given a local content and context for the consumers in different countries.

The question as to why and when international advertising can best become standardized is one that occupies the marketers of many multinationals in this globalized world. But, when the marketing strategists look at these matters through their international glasses, is standardization the only thing they should be thinking about? In 2010, researchers Shoaming Zou and Yong Z Volz from the University of Missouri (USA) developed an interesting theory for global advertising. They not only defined precisely what global advertising is and what effect it has, but they also zoomed in on a number of important conditions that must exist before a company opts for a global marketing approach.[1]

Their Global Marketing Strategy (GMS) integrates three current but very different perspectives in a worldwide marketing approach. In other words, they argue that standardization is not the only factor that needs to be taken into account by multinationals when they are considering the development of transnational advertising campaigns. According to Zou and Volz, the global success of companies is also dependent upon their ability to maximize advantages in specific markets, while at the same time seeking to coordinate operations at the international level, so that beneficial synergies and economies of scale can be created. The success of a global marketing approach is further determined by whether the company is competing in the world's largest markets and whether it has the capacity to 'integrate', meaning switching resources from one market to 'feed' another market so that a competitive advantage can be generated.

Building on this integrated vision of marketing strategy, Zou and Volz also offer their own definition of global advertising: namely, the extent to which a multinational standardizes its advertising messages, copy/visualizations and media use, coordinates the process of developing and executing advertising campaigns, and integrates its advertising campaign objectives and strategies across country markets.

These three components – standardization, coordination and integration – are fundamental to their vision, but this does not necessarily mean that a multinational needs to implement the three elements equally.

Ready for a global advertising approach?

Of course, it would be foolish to think that every company and brand can reap the same level of reward from a global approach. Consequently, a global strategy is only appropriate for some multinationals, and not all of them. What are the most important criteria for a company when deciding whether or not to adopt such a global advertising strategy?

The starting point for the Zou and Volz theory is that both external market factors and internal company characteristics (such as processes, knowledge and information) are important for the stronger performance of the brand worldwide. Although the researchers do not claim to be exhaustive, they offer a list of key characteristics relating to the market environment in which international companies operate, which can pave the way for a successful global advertising approach.

Convergence of demand

Popular management literature (including *The World is Flat* by Thomas Friedman) frequently indicates that in more and more sectors there is now such a thing as a 'global consumer': a consumer who, wherever he or she may live, shows similar preferences and wants similar products and services. And globalization has indeed meant that demand and the requirements of consumers have converged worldwide, have become more uniform. This trend is particularly noticeable in sectors that are less subject to culture-specific preferences, such as (high) technology and trend-conscious sectors, with products like computers, mobile phones, electronics, pharmaceutical goods and banking. In 'older' sectors, such as clothing, food and leisure goods, the convergence is much less pronounced. Zou and Volz argue that the greater the convergence of demand, the greater the likely benefit of a global advertising approach for multinational companies.

Comparable advertising regulations

As a result of increasing globalization and the growth in international trade, in recent years governments around the world have been devoting attention to the more uniform regulation of commercial operations. And research suggests that this same trend is also evident with regard to the international regulation of advertising. Zou and Volz contend that the presence of similar advertising regulations in the different countries in which the multinational brand is active can also be regarded as a positive factor in favour of a global advertising approach. Moreover, in this field there is also a rapidly growing trend towards self-regulation in many companies and sectors (see Chapter 10).

The availability of media

The rapid pace of technological progress has meant that in recent years a variety of new media and carriers have appeared in quick succession. Even so, new media such as digital TV and mobile telephones are still not widely available in many (less-developed) countries, or are of inferior quality. For this reason, Zou and Volz suggest, as their third criterion for adopting a global advertising strategy, that the multinational's preferred forms of media must be reliably available in all the countries where it operates.

A comparable competitive position

Just as in recent years consumer demand has been subject to a process of globalization, so the competitive battle between companies is also being increasingly fought at the international level. Coca-Cola and Pepsi, Boeing and Airbus, Procter & Gamble and Unilever: they all compete with each other in many different countries. And in some sectors, there is also strong additional competition from local companies. When a company is active in numerous countries, it is therefore important before adopting a global advertising strategy, according to Zou and Volz, that its competitive position is comparable with its rivals.

Competence of the advertising agency

The researchers argue that the competence of the multinational's chosen advertising agency is a fourth important factor that needs to be considered before adopting a global marketing approach. Many companies rely exclusively on their partner agencies for the development and implementation of their international campaigns. And it is indeed true that many of these agencies have developed strong, worldwide networks. But this does not mean that they are all equally suited to guide their client companies through the minefield of global advertising. Competence in this context means more than an excellent knowledge of the markets in which the multinational operates; it also means possessing the necessary creativity for the planning and execution of the campaigns and the ability to support the company in the integration of its objectives and strategies on a world scale.

In addition to these external factors, there are also a number of internal factors specific to the company that can influence the decision to adopt a global advertising strategy – or not.

Global orientation

Increasing globalization has meant that in recent decades more and more companies have become active internationally, so that they no longer judge their performance on a market-by-market basis but on a world scale. The global orientation of a company is a first important internal criterion when assessing whether or not to adopt a global advertising approach. In globally oriented companies there will be less resistance from local subsidiaries to a global strategy of standardization, coordination and integration, so that the interests of the worldwide brand can more easily take precedence over local interests.

International experience

Not all multinationals have the same experience, knowledge or ability to do business abroad or to launch products onto the market at international level. Research has shown that companies with more international experience are better able to find synergies between different markets, more quickly understand the relationships between these markets, and are more skilful in searching for ways to standardize processes, coordinate markets and integrate strategies from different countries. Zou and Volz conclude that a multinational's level of international experience is a second important factor when considering the pros and cons of a global advertising approach.

Autonomy of local subsidiaries

Some companies that are active on a worldwide scale give more autonomy to their local subsidiaries than other companies. This can often include the manner in which local marketing and advertising strategies are developed and rolled out. For example, the local management in these more 'independent' subsidiaries may be given more freedom to launch local products and initiatives, determine local prices, conduct local promotion and publicity campaigns, etc. However, in recent times many multinationals have actually attempted to restrict the freedom of action of their local subsidiaries, since they see this as necessary to strengthening the uniform strategy of a global band. Research has again confirmed that less autonomous local subsidiaries are more inclined to easily follow a global marketing or advertising strategy. In contrast, the global approach will be much less effective for a multinational with strong and independent local subsidiaries.

Ability to build up brands

Companies that have the ability to build up one or more strong brands will be more inclined and more able to standardize advertising campaigns, co-ordinate their planning and execution, and integrate their overall advertising strategy. In short, they are better equipped to follow the option of a global advertising approach. The ability of international companies to successfully grow a brand is determined by the extent to which they understand the 'global' consumer, are capable of developing new products and bringing them to market, and are successful in promoting the brand and providing good service.

'A global brand must be high quality, trendy, modern and socially responsible.'

But does a global advertising approach actually lead to better results? Zou and Volz believe that it does. According to them, a global advertising approach contributes significantly to brand performance. And research has indeed shown that global consumers equate global brands with high quality, trendiness, modernity and social responsibility. A brand that per-forms strongly is a brand that is well-known worldwide, has a uniform and positive image, can generate loyalty in consumers in many different countries and has a strong customer base in markets around the globe. Zou and Volz argue that the performance of a brand is a key determin-ing factor for the competitive advantage of a multinational in the global market. In particular, they claim, it is vital for companies in trend-sensitive and high-tech sectors to develop strong brands linked to a global marketing strategy.

Finally in this section, it needs to be stressed that a choice in favour of a global advertising approach is also strongly influenced by the desire to generate economies of scale, with the overall reduction of costs that this implies.

FIGURE 6.1   Model for a global advertising approach

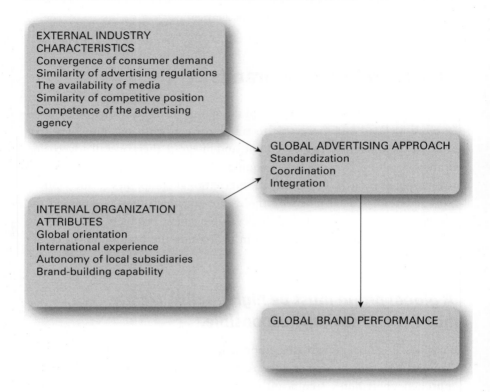

Internal and external factors strengthen the tendency towards a global approach to advertising. This approach results in greater standardization, coordination and integration of advertising strategy. Global brands are experienced by consumers as being high-quality, trendy, modern and socially responsible, particularly in high-tech and trend-sensitive sectors. However, there is also a counter-movement focused on local brand significance, reflecting cultural differences.

(Source: Zou and Volz, 2010)

Glocals and glaliens

The theory of Zou and Volz contends that it can be advantageous for some companies to develop a global brand on the basis of a global advertising strategy, providing that they attune their strategy to reflect a number of key internal and external factors. One of these factors is convergence of demand; namely, the extent to which it is possible to speak of global consumers with uniform preferences for products and brands. But to what extent does this really exist? Is it indeed possible to talk about global consumers? Or is the picture less clear-cut and more nuanced? Is the convergence of demand actually product and sector-dependent, as Zou and Volz suggest? Does the trend towards 'global' products and brands, backed by a global marketing strategy, really meet the demand and needs of consumers in different countries?

The respected marketing professors and researchers, Jan-Benedict Steenkamp and Martijn de Jong, went in search of the answers to these questions. They conducted a large-scale study that involved 13,000 respondents in 28 countries. Their results were published in the *Journal of Marketing* in November 2010.[2] They mapped out the different possible attitudes of consumers worldwide and assessed the drivers or values that determine consumer preference for local or global products. They took the term 'products' to means goods, services, brands, lifestyles and symbols.

First and foremost, their research revealed that the situation is indeed more complex than a straightforward division between consumers who opt for either local or global products. People who are positive towards local products do not necessarily reject global products, and vice versa. Steenkamp and de Jong distinguished four basic attitudes that consumers worldwide can display, independent of specific product categories:

- ✣ *Homogenization* – this is founded on the idea that in a globalized world many people will increasingly have a preference for global products, no matter where they live. This preference would be based on associations with success, progress, efficiency, etc. This is the attitude of the 'global consumer'.

- ✣ *Localization* is the opposite of homogenization. People with this attitude prefer local products to global products. The drivers underpinning this attitude are authenticity, traditionalism and an identification with a local lifestyle rather than a more international one.

- ✣ *Glocalization* – these are consumers who have a positive attitude towards both global and local products.

- ✣ *Glalienization* – consumers who have become disenchanted with contemporary consumer culture, whether it is local or global.

What makes a brand indispensible?

EURIB (European Institute for Brand Management) investigated the brands that Dutch consumers regard as being 'indispensible'. The publication of the results in 2012[3] allowed some interesting conclusions to be drawn:

TABLE 6.1 What makes a brand indispensible?

Position		Brand	Category	Indispensibility Score
2012	2011			
1	1	HEMA	Department store	74%
2	4	Albert Heijn	Supermarket	68%
3	2	Kruidvat	Chemist	66%
4	3	Bol.com	Webshop	65%
5	8	Blokker	Household store	65%
6	5	Ikea	Furniture store	64%
7	6	Google	Internet search engine	62%
8	7	NOS News	TV programme	62%
9	9	iDeal	Payment system	61%
10	11	Marktplaats	Internet auctioneer	60%

The top five indispensible brands in The Netherlands are HEMA, Albert Heijn, Kruidvat, Bol.com. and Blokker. And what do they have in common? They are all 'local' Dutch brands. The first conclusion from the research is therefore that a brand is perceived as being 'indispensible' when the public regards it as a cultural icon. In concrete terms, this means that the consumer inextricably associates the brand with the Dutch way of life, even to the extent of being willing to protest if there was a risk of the brand being withdrawn, as was the case with the popular Postbank, which was absorbed into ING in 2009.

A brand is also considered to be indispensible if it advertises extensively. But in addition to large-scale exposure to the brand, the consumer also expects a creative concept; a concept that catches not only the attention but also the imagination; in short, a concept the gives people something to talk about. In this respect, there is good reason why Albert Heijn and Bol.com are both in the top five.

The third conclusion of the EURIB study is that a brand is regarded as being indispensible if consumers can interact with it, if they can become a part of the brand. HEMA achieves this, for example, by giving consumers the chance to develop their own product in a design competition.

(Source: EURIB 2012)

Values determine consumer preferences

But what factors determine which of these four attitudes a consumer will have? Steenkamp and de Jong looked for possible explanations in the values that are important to people. Here, they once again distinguished three different value systems.

To begin with, there are national-cultural values. These are the convictions that people from the same land share about (more) abstract objectives and moral conduct, such as the dichotomy between 'the survival impulse' and 'self-expression' or 'traditional' and 'secular-rational'. Next, the researchers identified a set of general values or individual convictions relating to abstract objectives and moral conduct, such as security, power, stimulation and conformity. Finally, there are values specific to each different consumer, which can be linked to specific elements of their consumption, such as the product and the time or the (social and physical) space in which the product is consumed. These are values like 'materialism' (the idea that product consumption is a measure of success in life), 'neophilia' or 'the urge for innovation' (the idea that it is important to be amongst the first to buy a new product), 'nostalgia' (the idea that everything was better in the past), 'ethnocentrism' (where a person accepts and follows the norms of the group in which he or she lives) and 'environmentalism' (being concerned for nature and the environment).

On the basis of this three-tier framework, supplemented with socio-demographic parameters (gender, age, education, social class, civil status, income), the 13,000 respondents in 28 countries were asked to describe their attitude towards global and local products.

The first important conclusion reached by Steenkamp and de Jong was that it is indeed possible to speak of generalized attitudes to global and local products across different product categories. Using the three value systems and the socio-demographic factors, they were also able to identify the specific characteristics of the four basic consumer attitudes and profiles, as described above.

Consumers who prefer global products are in general younger, thrive on challenges and innovation, and are only mildly ethnocentric. They are not traditional and conformist, and their homogeneous attitude is more frequently found in secular-rational societies.

Consumers who prefer local products are in general older and more ethnocentric. They value traditions and are conformist by nature. Their localized attitude is more common in traditional cultures.

'Glocal' consumers – who embrace both global and local products – generally have the profile of a forward-looking woman, who is fairly materialistic. This is an attitude more likely to be valued in the so-called 'survival' societies, where the level of individual choice and freedom in economic, social and cognitive terms is more limited.

'Glalien' consumers – who have become totally disenchanted with all aspects of consumerism, whether local or global – generally have the profile of a nostalgic man, who is not materialistic and who lives in a society where happiness, quality of life and environmental protection are regarded as more important than consumption.

A nuanced picture

A technology company like Apple rolls out the same brand and the same product worldwide. In contrast, PepsiCo allows its consumers in different countries to develop their own flavours for its Lay's brand of potato chips. In both cases the approach is successful.

What conclusions did Steenkamp and de Jong reach for companies that are active in the global economy?

In the first place, they warned against placing too much emphasis on global brands in the company strategy. A portfolio that combines global and local brands is often a much better way for brands to reach their desired target groups. Moreover, companies that are internationally active need to better adjust their global positioning to more closely reflect the attitudes of consumers in different countries. For example, Thai consumers (like US consumers) have a strong preference for domestically manufactured products, while the Germans, Swiss and Irish have a more a positive attitude towards global products than to local ones. Even within a regional market like Eastern Europe, there are radically different approaches to the global–local issue amongst the various countries.

As far as global account management is concerned – ie, the coherent management of matters such as price-setting, positioning, service and product specifications, etc at an international level – Steenkamp and de Jong recommend that multinationals should take account of the attitudes that local people adopt to both global and local products, adjusting their local approach where necessary.

As for the local companies that need to compete against these international giants, they can attempt to more fully exploit their local cultural relevance in the hope of gaining a competitive advantage. A good example is the successful marketing of traditional abbey-made beers in Belgium, in what is a very competitive market environment. These beers are a classic case, combining local authenticity with the skilful use of a premium positioning.

In addition to cultural values, Steenkamp and de Jong emphasize the importance of socio-demographic factors in determining attitudes towards global and local products. These factors explain people's attitudes just as well (in the case of local products) or even better (in the case of global products) than the general consumer values.

Summary

Not all companies and brands will benefit in the same manner (if at all) from a global advertising approach. A global strategy is certainly a good idea for some multinationals, but not for all of them. If handled correctly, this kind of global approach can result in a brand that performs strongly worldwide, but only if the approach is adjusted to take account of key external factors and internal company characteristics.

Global brands are not the be-all and end-all of everything. Unquestionably, they have great potential, but are not a passport to automatic commercial success. Although it is possible to speak of a global consumer attitude, multinationals nevertheless still need to take account of other consumer profiles, such as glocals and glaliens.

Companies that are internationally active are therefore best advised to adjust their global positioning strategy to reflect the different attitudes of consumers in different countries. In addition to value systems, socio-demographic factors play an important role in determining consumer attitudes towards global and local brands.

Practical inspiration

1 Make an analysis of the relative contributions of global and local brands to the portfolio of an international company.

2 Why do worldwide brands opt for a glocal advertising strategy?

3 What is the most effective strategy for a high-tech brand – and why?

4 What are the advantages and disadvantages of a global versus a local advertising strategy?

5 Give examples of the glalienization phenomenon in different sectors. What are the consequences for brands?

CASE STUDY Chrysler: 'Imported from Detroit'

By winning a Grand Effie in North America in 2012, Chrysler claimed the top prize for its comeback following bankruptcy in 2009. Consumers and manufacturers had turned their backs on the US auto industry and Chrysler had to tackle the problem of the very low level of loyalty that was left amongst the public. That is why the brand aimed not only to sell its 200 model, but also the category. The campaign repositioned the US brand with US values, in an US town, using US idol Eminem. And it was a PR triumph: within the first 24 hours, the spot was viewed more than 4 million times on YouTube. Chrysler sales skyrocketed: in one month, sales more than tripled. Despite Chrysler's successes, the city of Detroit nonetheless filed for bankruptcy in July 2013.

SOURCE Effie Worldwide (2012). Chrysler. Imported from Detroit. Consulted online: www.effie.org

Notes

1   Zou, S and Volz, Y Z (2010) An integrated theory of global advertising: an application of the GMS theory, *Journal of Advertising Research*, **29** (1), pp 97–111

2   Steenkamp, J B E M and de Jong, M G (2010) A global investigation into the constellation of consumer attitudes towards global and local products, *Journal of Marketing*, **74**, pp 18–40

3   EURIB (2012) Top 100 indespensible brands in 2012 [Online] http://www.eurib.org/top-100-onmisbare-merken-2013-html

07

Conscience or cash?

Under pressure from greater social awareness about the need for sustainable entrepreneurship, many brands have undergone a major transition in their marketing and advertising campaigns. In many cases this has been to strengthen the corporate reputation of their company or brand, but also frequently to communicate the development of new 'green' products and services to their consumers. Of course, the aim remains the same: to increase turnover and profits. But is there a large group of consumers actually waiting to buy these green products and services? In these difficult economic times, might it not be that price and functionality are the most persuasive purchase arguments? And what can brands do to avoid appearing hypocritical?

The 1990s saw the first major wave of companies that were anxious to play the 'green card' in their marketing and advertising campaigns. This coincided with greater public awareness and greater media attention on the environment and the need to protect it, particularly in the Western world. And the phenomenon of green marketing and advertising is still a 'live' issue today. Just think of McDonald's' recent launch of a green logo in Europe, or H&M's collections in organic cotton, or the Nissan Leaf, or the sustainable Triodos Bank.

The CSR paradox

As said, green marketing and advertising can be seen as instruments to strengthen a company's reputation and/or to promote green products and services. The efforts that a company makes in terms of greater sustainability and environmental friendliness are generally referred to as socially responsible enterprise (SRE) or corporate social responsibility (CSR).

In their article *The Catch 22 of Communicating CSR*,[1] a group of Danish researchers, including Professor Majken Schultz, looked at the challenges facing Western companies in terms of their wish to communicate their socially responsible and sustainable policies in a correct and balanced way. On the one hand, the public expects companies to operate in a socially responsible manner. On the other hand, they are suspicious when companies communicate their social responsibility too loudly and too explicitly. Research has shown that the companies that are most active in the field of CSR are also the companies that are most critically monitored by consumer groups, journalists and NGOs. This, as the Danish research team point out, is the paradox of CSR.

This conclusion is also important in light of the results of separate research into the 'Americanization' of European CSR strategies. US companies are more outspoken and more explicit in their CSR communication, because the expectations in terms of social commitment are much higher in the United States than in Europe.

How can companies best deal with this CSR paradox? The Danish researchers developed an approach for balanced CSR communication. In the first place, they argue for a so-called 'inside-out' strategy. Their research showed that involving the staff in the company's CSR policy and securing their commitment to that policy is essential as a basis for credible CSR communication. This means that companies should first focus on CSR measures that impact on the staff themselves. Only then should they move on to efforts that can benefit the outside world, starting with local communities and then building up to national and (later) international stakeholders. Schultz and her team also argue in favour of a combination of direct (more explicit) and indirect (more implicit) methods for CSR communication. The direct communication should not be targeted at the general public through large advertising campaigns, but should be focused on a select group of 'experts', such as journalists, politicians, government bodies and NGOs. These third parties will then take on the task of indirectly communicating the company's CSR policy to the wider public and the company's customers. This approach allows companies to communicate explicitly in an implicit manner. It adds an objective filter to the communication process, so that the CSR message is more credible when circulated by the 'impartial' third parties. Even so, warns the research team, this does not mean that companies can avoid the CSR paradox completely. As a result, companies still need to operate with the necessary sensitivity and sophistication to strengthen their corporate image through the correct and skilful implementation of their CSR policy.

In Belgium, the leading discount retailer Colruyt is one of the companies that has understood this message – and understood it well. The company does not conduct large-scale campaigns to show how green and sustainable its operations are. Instead, their marketing communications for the general public concentrate on price and products. But when the supermarket is the first in the country to open hydrogen tanking facilities for environmentally friendly cars – an event attended by various politicians and well covered in the media – the CSR message nonetheless also filters down to the ordinary man and woman in the street. This is the kind of 'balance' meant by the Danish research team: finding the right, indirect channels to reach the right, limited target group, thereby avoiding the charge of 'corporate hypocrisy'. Above all, it is a question of 'saying what we do' and 'doing what we say'.

How to avoid corporate hypocrisy

As previously mentioned, companies are nowadays increasingly assessed and evaluated in terms of their social responsibility. In a globalized world, in which information is more widely and more quickly available than ever before and business processes are becoming more complex and more difficult to control, it is inevitable that more reports about incidents of socially irresponsible behaviour will make the news.

It was in their 2009 research study, which received the 'Best Published Paper Award' from Oxford University's Centre for Corporate Reputation, that professors Tilmann Wagner, Richard Lutz and Barton Weitz first introduced the term 'corporate hypocrisy'.[2] By this they meant the public perception that a company likes to portray itself in the most positive light, to show things as being 'better' than they really are. This is a negative perception which means that customers and consumers are less convinced about the social responsibility of the company, which in turn can negatively influence their attitude towards that company and its brand(s).

How can companies avoid their CSR communication being seen as hypocritical by customers and the general public, particularly when an incident occurs or the public are confronted with external reports that conflict with what the company is saying?

The research carried out by Wagner, Lutz and Weitz focused on three possible dilemmas that confront companies when they are devising a strategy to avoid the risk of negative image-forming in the event of potentially damaging incidents or reporting of socially irresponsible behaviour:

✤ Is there any difference in impact if the CSR communication strategy is proactive or reactive?

✤ Does the public act differently if information is abstract or concrete?

✤ Does it help to try to anticipate an incident with communication that softens the blow and offers counterarguments?

A proactive communication strategy for CSR implies that a company disseminates information to create an image of social responsibility before any incident has occurred or negative reports about its activities have appeared. A reactive communication strategy implies that a company only communicates about its social responsibility to protect its image once an incident or negative reporting has already happened. The Wagner-Lutz-Weitz research revealed that once a company's socially irresponsible behaviour becomes known, the public regards companies with a proactive CSR communication strategy as more hypocritical than companies that only communicate reactively once the news of an incident has broken. In other words, too much proactive CSR communication can have a negative impact in crisis situations.

The research also confirmed a second hypothesis; namely, that companies can optimize their proactive and reactive strategies and minimize the potential perception of corporate hypocrisy by making their CSR communication more abstract or more concrete, depending on the circumstances. An abstract message, for example, might be limited to a short declaration that the company is strongly committed to the protection of the environment. A more concrete message might describe in more detail precisely how the company is protecting the environment through its recycling programme, water conservation measures, etc (see Chapter 10). The researchers concluded that the use of concrete messages in a proactive communication strategy strengthens the public perception of hypocrisy, while in a reactive strategy concrete messages can actually help to reduce that perception. The key is to 'under-promise and over-deliver'. If you are not certain that you can keep your promises, it is better not to make any. If you make them and don't keep them, the charge of hypocrisy will inevitably follow.

'*If you are not certain that you can keep your promises, it is better not to make any*'

Finally, the research showed that companies, irrespective of their communication strategy (proactive or reactive), are seen as less hypocritical when they provide the public in advance of any expected incident or adverse reporting with mildly negative information and counterarguments as a precautionary measure. This is the so-called 'resistance theory'. The company acknowledges the bad news and puts it into perspective, while at the same time reconfirming its full commitment to a socially responsible policy.

Sustainable consumers don't exist

Between 2008 and 2010, the Greendex – the sustainable consumption index compiled by National Geographic and Globescan – showed an increasing sustainability trend in 17 countries. In 2012, there was actually a fall in most of these countries for the first time in recent years. The problems of the continuing economic crisis are clearly more important in consumer thinking than concerns for the environment. Most surveys show that there is still much work to be done in the field of sustainability awareness.

What motivates consumers to consume 'sustainably'? Do they really care more about the planet than other people or are they driven by financial considerations? Do 'green consumers' actually exist?

At first sight, there is no simple explanation for sustainable consumer behaviour. The Futures Company, an international consultancy that investigates and predicts trends, has conducted specific research into green consumption. Their results show that the environment is not a high priority for many green consumers and is not the primary driver for their purchase behaviour.[3] When people buy sustainably, the environment is just one of many factors that influence their purchasing decision, alongside personal considerations like cost-cutting, quality time with the children, etc. The truth is that the term 'sustainable consumption' means different things to different people – and these definitions can vary quite widely. There is no single vision of a sustainable lifestyle and consequently there is no such thing as a 'sustainable consumer'.

In 2010, The Futures Company conducted a survey in 20 countries to chart the different types of consumers on the basis of their engagement towards the concept of sustainability. This resulted in the following six profiles:

✤ *Pioneers*: this is the most engaged group of consumers, who are intrinsically convinced by the green philosophy. They are interested in the benefits of green, but first need to see the proof (15 per cent).

✤ *Adopters*: this group is also engaged, like the pioneers, but more as a result of social pressure from friends and media than from absolute conviction. They like to show that they are 'green' (21 per cent).

✤ *Strugglers*: this group is motivated, but sees a number of practical problems with the green lifestyle. For them, access to and the ease of sustainable behaviour are key factors (13 per cent).

✤ *Confused*: this group is reasonably motivated, but they have the feeling that they cannot make a difference or are being fed contradictory information. For them, actions with a clear and tangible result are crucial (12 per cent).

✤ *Passives*: this group is indifferent about matters relating to the green lifestyle and the environment in general. They will only 'buy green' if there is a clear benefit for themselves (16 per cent).

✤ *Sceptics*: this group is not environmentally unfriendly, but they do not believe that the environmental situation is as bad as some people claim (23 per cent).

If left to the consumers alone, The Futures Company does not expect any major changes in the relative size of these six groups in the near future. Change will only occur if important measures or strong incentives are imposed from outside. Consequently, they underline the need for marketers to be aware of the level of green commitment in their specific target groups.

The Futures Company goes on to argue that value, ease of use and performance still largely determine the choice of product at the point of sale. But their research further showed that a new catalyst for green consumption is also emerging, a catalyst that is popular with consumers of all kinds: 'the fight against waste'. This is a criterion that is always likely to appeal during periods of economic recession. As such, it could play an important role in the short term.

Green advertising works

If consumers do not regard green as their top priority and if there is no such thing as a 'green consumer', is there any real point in green marketing and green advertising? And what exactly is 'green advertising'?

Consumers often find the claims made by green advertising vague and unconvincing. In fact, the lack of clarity about the 'real' intentions of the companies who launch green ads and campaigns has created scepticism amongst consumers around the world. Nevertheless, a number of recent research studies have shown that green advertising can work – providing it focuses in the correct way on the reality of a very diverse and 'conditioned' consumer.[4]

To understand how consumers react to or are convinced by green advertisements, it is necessary to examine the term 'green advertising' more closely, breaking it down into its component parts. Green advertising can be defined as 'making publicity for a product or brand through the use of environmentally related claims or arguments'. There are two types of claims: informative (or substantive) claims and affective (or associative) claims (see Chapter 5).

Informative claims offer information about concrete, tangible advantages and characteristics of the product or brand, which are able to convince the consumer to consider making a green purchase. This claim might relate, for example, to the smaller ecological footprint of the product or brand or the fact that the product is made from 'natural' substances. (Typically, this information is summarized in the message or 'copy' of the ad.) With informative claims, the process that convinces the consumer is a cognitive one. The consumer is persuaded to make a purchase on the basis of hard arguments. Various recent studies into the cognitive processes involved in green advertising have shown that the strategy of trying to convince consumers on the basis of cognitive arguments actually does work. Or it does, assuming that the consumer feels more strongly engaged by environmental aspects as a result of a greater environmental awareness in society at large. In this respect, research results have indicated that clear and specific arguments are not only far more convincing than vague claims, but that they also have a positive effect on purchasing intentions and lead to an improved attitude towards the brand.[5]

However, another recent research project into the different attitudes of consumers to environmental awareness concluded that 'ambivalent' green consumers – in other words, green consumers who have contradictory feelings about environmental awareness – react differently to the claims made in green advertisements. It seems that ads with strong green claims can make these 'doubting' consumers feel uncomfortable. As a result, they process the ad in a 'prejudicial' manner. This is known as 'motivated processing'. Their own suspicion and distrust undermines the credibility of the ad, influences their product evaluation and reduces their appreciation of the brand.[6]

But informative claims are only part of the story. Green advertising also makes use of **associative or affective claims**. These are claims that suggest an association with the environment in a less obvious, less tangible manner. The use of 'natural' scenes and images in advertising is a good example of this approach. But to what purpose? Are there emotional processes that can be triggered by the affective claims in green advertising, processes that have a positive effect on product and brand perception?

Putting green in the picture

In 2009, Patrick Hartmann and Vanessa Apaolaza-Ibáñez of the University of the Basque Country published the results of their research study that attempted to answer this question.[7] The report described how the number of 'nature images' used in advertising had increased significantly in recent times. These images are used to evoke calm and beauty. For consumers, nature stands for 'real', 'good' and 'authentic' things, values and traditions, but also for family intimacy, companionship and pleasure. Nature (in the form of travelling, getting away from it all), the countryside and even the more controlled natural environment of the garden are all used to draw a sharp contrast with the hustle and bustle of city life and work.

According to the Spanish researchers, this frequent use of natural images should come as no surprise. The power of its attraction is rooted deep in human behaviour. The emotional affinity that people have for nature is well documented. Various scientific studies into human health support the hypothesis that 'nature' in its broadest sense is good for our physical and psychological well-being. In other words, people are 'naturally' attracted to nature. There is even a research study which has shown that people have a preference for relatively open, peaceful landscapes; a preference that some experts attribute to the fact that in days gone by this type of landscape was more advantageous for hunting and the gathering of food, on which our ancestors depended for their survival.

In short, there are many indicators to support the claim that contact with nature can lead to positive emotional experiences and even induce certain modes of behaviour – according to Hartmann and Apaolaza-Ibáñez. These emotional experiences can be the result of direct contact with nature, such as smelling the fragrances of the forest. But the research duo demonstrated that they can also be activated by images of nature broadcast in commercial media. They referred to this phenomenon as 'virtual nature experiences'.

Their conclusions were based on the testing of 360 respondents from Madrid, Barcelona, Bilbao, Vitoria and San Sebastian. They were each shown a series of short experimental ads for five different brands in different product categories, including mobile telephones, cars, petrol and washing powders. There were three different types of ad per brand. The first showed the product against a neutral background, supported by a description of the product characteristics that did not focus on environmental aspects. The second showed the product against the same neutral background, but this time using a description of product characteristics that did focus on environmental aspects and also adding a 'natural-sounding' name (for example, the Nokia GreenMotion instead of the Nokia 7370). The third ad showed the same environmentally named product in a beautiful natural setting. Once they had seen the ads, the respondents were asked to fill in a questionnaire, which sought to evaluate their perception of the environmental product characteristics of the brands, and also their attitude towards those brands.

In the first place, the results showed that the advertisements offering information about the specific environmentally friendly characteristics of the products resulted in a better overall attitude amongst the respondents towards the brand, precisely because of the associations evoked by those characteristics. In addition, it was also clear that the use of natural images in advertisements can induce emotional experiences that are comparable (up to a certain point) with the direct experience of nature in the wild. This led on to the most important conclusion of the study; namely, that the adequate use of these virtual nature experiences can have a significantly better impact on the attitude of the viewer towards the brand than the straightforward use of informational claims unsupported by natural images.

In other words, a positive attitude towards brands, green consumption and even environmentally friendly behaviour can all be stimulated by virtual nature experiences induced by the use of natural images in green advertising. Does this mean that from now on every brand will pack its advertisements with shots of green trees and blue skies? Probably not, since this would lead to the counter-productive danger of 'greenwashing'. In this respect, a number of initiatives have already been launched to monitor and assess green ads in relation to the real green engagement of companies concerned, with the results being published online.

A good example is the Greenwashing Index, set up by the University of Oregon, in collaboration with EnviroMedia Social Marketing and the Stopgreenwash website of Greenpeace. If the ads are misleading or hypocritical, the company risks being pilloried in public (see Chapter 10).

Reputation as the icing on the cake

Can companies demonstrate their ethical intentions and actions to their customers in a manner that also supports their commercial objectives? Companies are increasingly coming to realize that their reputation is an important element in their overall value, and one that can have a positive impact on their results. This reputation is influenced by a variety of factors, but in turn it influences other key aspects of the company and its operations.

Researchers Gatti and Snehota from the Università della Svizzera italiana and Caruana from the University of Malta looked specifically at the way perceptions about social responsibility, ethical trade and product quality not only influence the reputation of a brand, but also the purchase intentions of consumers. Their findings appeared in the *Journal of Brand Management* in January 2012.[8]

They tested their hypotheses on a sample population drawn from the consumers of two brands of the typical Italian Christmas cake, the *panettone*. The two brands are well known in a specific cultural and geographical region and one of them is famed for its strong commitment to CSR. The results of the research show that the perception of a company as being socially responsible has a direct effect on that company's reputation and also has a positive impact on the intentions of consumers to purchase its products. A direct link between the perception of product quality and purchasing intentions was also shown.

This led the researchers to conclude that brand managers should not only concentrate on maintaining product quality, but should also seek to exploit the opportunities presented by the development of CSR activities for the enhancement of the company's reputation. In particular, the researchers suggested that marketers should focus on three aspects. In the first place, they must focus on the commercial aspect; in other words, advertising that emphasizes honesty in relation to product quality through the provision of correct and sincere information about the characteristics and qualities of the product range. This will also serve to strengthen the perception of product quality. Secondly, they need to ensure that they behave ethically in their dealings with their customers and in the pursuit of their business objectives. Finally, they must not lose sight of the need to develop initiatives that demonstrate their commitment to social responsibility and the environment, and they must communicate these initiatives in an appropriate way.

Summary

Involving your own staff right from the very beginning is crucial for the success of CSR communication. A proactive or reactive CSR communication strategy has different implications. If a company communicates too much proactively about CSR, it will be regarded as more hypocritical by the public when it finds itself in a negative CSR situation. Indirect communication via opinion-makers can often be a better strategy. Remember that abstract CSR messages work better in a proactive communication strategy and concrete CSR messages are more appropriate for a reactive strategy.

Remember also that there is no such thing as 'the sustainable consumer'. Consumers have many widely differing views about sustainability. The use of nature images in advertising can strengthen the positive attitude of consumers towards a product or brand and can also stimulate green consumption and environmentally friendly behaviour. But watch out for 'greenwashing': companies have to mean what they say; otherwise, they will soon be exposed as hypocritical.

Practical inspiration

1 Involve your own staff right from the very start in your CSR campaign.

2 How does your brand deal with its stakeholders?

3 What are the pitfalls for brands when communicating about sustainable enterprise?

4 Devise a campaign strategy that will help you to avoid charges of hypocrisy with regard to corporate social responsibility.

5 What role can 'green' play in the advertising of your brand?

CASE STUDY   American Express: 'Small Business Saturday'

Conscience goes beyond green advertising. Stepping up for someone, something someplace can certainly pay off for brands. In 2010, American Express created Small Business Saturday, a new shopping day between Black Friday and Cyber Monday, to support small businesses in their bid to attract more clients, create jobs, preserve neighbourhoods and – in essence – fuel local economies nationwide. In 2011, the challenge was to transform this 'one-shot' into a permanent fixture. And it worked: over 500,000 small businesses participated and transactions on the day rose by 23 per cent. In the end, 103 million Americans 'shopped small', including President Obama, and the day was declared an official day on the US shopping calendar. Not surprisingly, the awards followed: a Grand Prix at the Cannes Lions in 2012 and a golden North American Effie in 2013.

SOURCE Effie Worldwide (2013). American Express. Small Business Saturday. Consulted online: www.effie.org

Notes

1   Morsing, M, Schultz, M and Nielsen, K U (2008) The Catch 22 of
    communicating CSR, *Journal of Marketing Communications*, **14** (2),
    pp 97–111

2   Wagner, T, Lutz, R J and Weitz, B A (2009) Corporate hypocrisy: overcoming
    the threat of inconsistent CSR perceptions, *Journal of Marketing*, **73**,
    pp 77–91

3   Walton, F, The Futures Company (2010) Pragmatic environmentalism,
    Admap, **45** (10), pp 28–30

4   Hartman, P and Apaolaza-Ibáñez, V (2009) Green advertising revisited,
    International Journal of Advertising, **28** (4), pp 715–39

5   See 4

6   Chang, C (2012) Feeling ambivalent about green, *Journal of Advertising*,
    40 (4), pp 19–32

7   See 4 and 5

8   Gatti, L, Caruana, A and Snehota, I (2012) The role of corporate social
    responsibility, perceived quality and corporate reputation on purchase
    intention: implications for brand management, *Journal of Brand
    Management*, **20** (1), pp 65–76

08

Old or new?

In uncertain economic times many brands look back to the past. In this way, they wish to demonstrate to the buying public that they are durable, authentic and sustainable. Research shows that brands with a 'history' evoke powerful emotional associations in consumers. However, other research indicates that brands need to do more than simply recycle their glorious past. It is important that brands continue to invest in innovation and user-friendliness, since this will give consumers precisely what they want: the best of both worlds.

The US comedian George Carlin has been claiming for years that society is dominated by what he calls 'yestermania'. This is an excessive attachment to the past.

> Our culture is composed of sequels, reruns, remakes, revivals, reissues, re-releases, recreations, re-enactments, adaptations, anniversaries, memorabilia, oldies radio and nostalgia record collections.[1]

This attachment to the past is also gaining ground in the advertising world. Old TV commercials are being dusted off, revamped and re-broadcast, such as the Mars ad, where a young man knocks on the door of a monastery after a broken romance, but suddenly finds the desire and energy to face the world again after a bite of his favourite chocolate bar. The trash can full of Mars wrappers suggests that this is not the first time this has happened. Nor was it the first time for Mars: the original commercial dates from the beginning of the 1990s. The only difference 20 years later was new background music and a more raunchy ex-girlfriend in the young man's photo.

In much the same way, the discontinued 'mascots' of yesteryear are also being resurrected. Chiquita Banana is a good international example, while in The Netherlands the HAK brand has recalled the legendary (in Holland, at least) Martine Bijl to star in its TV ads. This is a tried-and-tested advertising strategy, and one that has proved its worth on more than one occasion in the past. At the start of the 1980s, new life was blown into the flagging Levi Strauss jeans brand, with an unashamedly nostalgic campaign, including the music.

Newer brands can also achieve the same effect, but in a slightly different manner. Part of the success of the relatively new Bops Potato Chips is attributable to its 'vintage' style packaging. Other, more-longstanding brands, such as Coca-Cola and Mars, prefer to focus on the unbroken continuity of their products. A good way to do this is by celebrating anniversaries: Mars has celebrated its birthday in many countries, Coca-Cola recently honoured its 125 years and Bacardi partied for 150 years. Some brands even create a history – and consumers are happy to believe them. The popular US clothing brand Hollister has the date '1922' on all its products, even though the brand was only founded in 2001 as an offshoot of the more famous Abercrombie & Fitch. In other words, retro is 'in'. But does it really add as much value as the advertisers think it does?

Nostalgia in uncertain times

In today's modern world, characterized as it is by uncertainty and crisis, we are more often inclined to look back to the 'good old days', recalling memories of the past, when everything seemed 'better'. In turbulent times, nostalgia can offer a feeling of comfort. This, of course, is nothing new. Consider, for example, the wave of nostalgia that swept over the world around the turn of the century. Marketing professor Barbara Stern (Rutgers, The State University of New Jersey) has called this the *fin-de-siècle* effect: the tendency people have to look back whenever the end of a century is approaching.[2] At the same time, it is also an indication that people want to 'wipe the slate clean' and start again. 'Out with the old, in with the new.'

A combination of these elements – the socio-economic crisis, the *fin-de-siècle* effect, and the increasing unpredictability of consumer preferences – has led to a kind of retro revolution in marketing and advertising. New life is being breathed into old brands, brands that remind us of better and happier days in the past.[3]

In the eyes of the consumer, the history of a brand – even if it has disappeared from the scene for a time (like the Mini Cooper) or even if the history is 'fake' (like Hollister) – represents a kind of reliability. These nostalgic brands evoke various associations and each association has its own emotional connection. In this way, there is potential for the more effective registration and even activation of brand information.

But not everyone sees it this way. At the opposite end of the marketing spectrum we have the counter-theory of 'neo-nostalgia', put forward by Fredric Jameson, one of the most important theoreticians of post-modernism. He claims that nostalgia has nothing to do with emotion, but is more a kind of aesthetic reaction to the past.[4] Our nostalgia is activated by external stimuli, such as classic slogans, names and packaging.

'The definition of 'nostalgia' that will be used in this chapter was first coined by marketing professor Morris Holbrook (The Columbia Business School of New York): 'a sentimental yearning for a product or experience from the past'.[5]

Nostalgia is commercially attractive because it can influence the mood of the consumer in a positive manner. It makes the consumer happier. We see this happening around us all the time, in our everyday life: people are always looking for ways to make themselves feel better, by modulating their own mood. In this sense, our mood is both cause and consequence. But a mood is not the same as an emotion. A mood is less intense, is longer (on average) and is usually experienced unconsciously, in the sense that it does not require any direct link with an object/cause. In contrast, emotions are more intense, shorter in duration and do require the stimulus of a direct link with an object/cause. An example: when someone is wrestling with the emotion of sadness, he or she is usually sad about something specific, such as a personal loss; but when someone is in a sad mood, this does not necessarily need to be connected to any specific object or cause, but is more a case of being sad 'in general' (as opposed to 'in particular').

Emotions imply a certain understanding of something. Cognition is therefore necessary before we can experience emotions. This is not the case with moods, which do not require knowledge, cause or object. Consequently, a mood is a general rather than a specific condition.

'There is evidence that nostalgic brands – thanks to the stimulation of positive moods – can encourage purchase behaviour.'

The German professor Ulrich Orth (Christian Albrechts University) and the Austrian lecturer Steffi Gal (St. Pölten University) have recently published the results of their experimental research into the relationship between nostalgic brands and consumer moods and, in particular, the effect that this relationship can have on purchase behaviour.[6] Fifty respondents were asked to complete a test in a room with pleasant background music; 51 others were asked to complete the test in a room with sad background music. Before the test started, all 101 respondents were required to describe their 'mood' under the influence of the music. They were then shown stimulus material from both nostalgic and non-nostalgic brands from three different categories (body care, perfume, confectionery). They were asked to evaluate the extent to which these stimuli evoked nostalgic memories and had an effect on their mood and their purchase intentions.

Before the experiment, Orth and Gal assumed that the nostalgic brands would have a stronger, more positive effect on the mood of consumers than the non-nostalgic brands. They thought that consumers make purchases as an expression of the need to improve or repair their mood. These hypotheses were confirmed by the results of their empirical research: there is evidence that nostalgic brands – thanks to the stimulation of positive moods – can encourage purchase behaviour.

The researchers also formulated a number of other hypotheses, in which they assumed that the encouragement of purchase behaviour first requires the consumer to have a degree of knowledge and hope. Some people have a greater need for knowledge. They are more comfortable with tasks that require them to process information and they obtain pleasure from the cognitive effort that this involves. Other people are more intuitive and pragmatic, and therefore have a lesser need for knowledge. The Orth and Gal research showed that the moods of consumers with a high knowledge requirement are more positively influenced by nostalgic brands than consumers with a low knowledge requirement. The researchers went on to identify 'hope' as the stimulating parameter for the positive moods created by the nostalgic brands. Hope is a positive attitude, an expectation that something good will happen, even though that something is uncertain and lies in the future. In this respect, the test results showed that individuals with more hope are more positively influenced by nostalgic brands than individuals with less hope.

What general conclusions can be drawn from this experiment? Nostalgic brands, through their associations with nostalgic memories, can influence the moods of consumers. This is particularly the case for consumers who have plenty of hope and a high requirement for knowledge. Moreover, this positive mood in turn has a positive effect on purchase behaviour. This led Orth and Gal to draw a further conclusion; namely, that a nostalgic strategy targeted at consumers in a less positive mood has potential to succeed. Many of today's brand managers also seem to have grasped this point (in part, at least), as witnessed by the numerous nostalgic advertising campaigns that encourage consumers to escape from their negative moods by returning to the better times of the past, even if only in their imaginations.

Furthermore, another study – a 2012 collaboration between researchers from Cornell University, the University of Washington and Old Dominion University – also confirms that nostalgia has a positive impact on attitudes towards the advertisement and on the bonding with the brand. One of their main conclusions is that nostalgic ads work better than non-nostalgic ones, even among the less loyal – light – consumers.[7]

These research findings allow marketers to better position their nostalgic brands, at least in terms of time and their choice of points of sale, since these can be arranged to coincide with the moments when the target consumers are likely to be in a less positive mood. In addition, a better understanding about which consumers (in terms of characteristics) are more likely to buy a nostalgic brand makes it possible to select target groups and attract potential buyers more efficiently.

Modern retro

This all leads on to another important question. Is it enough for a brand simply to put consumers at their ease and stimulate a better mood? Or should they be trying to inspire their consumers as well?

It has been claimed that nostalgic brands and their related advertising seek to exploit the nostalgia of a particular generation. The strange thing is that even consumers who do not belong to that generation – and perhaps have never even heard of the original product or brand – can also be swept along on the same wave of stimulated nostalgia. And this is something that marketers and advertisers also understand.

The US clothing brand Banana Republic designed a *Mad Men* capsule collection (limited to just 10 items) for the domestic market. *Mad Men* is a popular and award-winning HBO television series that evokes the golden advertising years of the 1960s. This is an era that is largely unknown to most of the programme's viewers, but it still appeals to them, precisely because it makes them yearn for the (so-called) 'better times' of the past. Banana Republic's 'Man Men' collection sold like the proverbial hot cakes, and not only to women who were old enough to have experienced the 1960s for themselves.

Instagram is another example. We have moved on from vague, blurred photos and now live in an age of sharply defined, digital images, but with Instagram we happily return to the age of indistinct, fuzzy visual effects. If it is old, it must be relevant. And if it is relevant, it must have some important meaning.

Old brands inspire the younger generations by offering them a mix of the elements that most appeal to the young: a familiar and reliable brand combined with the latest state-of-the-art characteristics. If brands wish to appeal to a broad, primarily young, public, they must be able to blend the retro element with the requirements of the modern world. This is the phenomenon known as retro branding.[8]

Retro branding involves bringing an old, well-known brand up to date, by giving it new characteristics without losing its old identity. It is the renewal or re-launching of a product or service from an earlier period, but in a modernized form that satisfies the needs of today's consumers. In other words, it is both old-fashioned and brand new. These retro brands are not the same as nostalgic brands. In nostalgic brands, the original products remain largely untouched; in retro brands, they are given a complete make-over.

Nostalgic and retro brands do, however, have some things in common. They both seek to generate part of their persuasive power from the associations with the past they evoke in consumers. As long ago as 1979, Fred Davis distinguished two types of associations: on the one hand, there are personal associations, related to the personal life of the individual consumer; and on the other hand, there are common or generational associations, related to social changes in the environment or the spirit of the times.[9] Retro brands can play on both these types. This was described by researchers Eleonora Cattaneo (SDA Bocconi) and Carolina Guerini (LIUC) as 'brand heritage'.

Brand heritage is the inheritance of a brand, or all the associations from the past that can be linked to that brand.[10] However, there was no empirical evidence to show that the use of these past associations produced any better results than other brand associations, such as product specifications. Cattaneo and Guerini decided to go in search of this evidence and in 2012 started an empirical research study into the relationship between a retro branding strategy and consumer preference for a retro brand.

They tested two basic hypotheses. Their first assumption was that exposure to retro brands would evoke nostalgic and emotional associations in consumers, with a positive effect on consumer preference for a retro brand (to the detriment of 'new' brands). In this respect, marketing professor David Aaker had already argued in 1996 that the rejuvenation of an old brand could be facilitated by the clever use of associations that could be linked to the roots of the brand.[11] The second hypothesis assumed that a retro brand cannot simply be re-launched in its original form, but needs to be updated with new and more modern functions.

These hypotheses were examined on the basis of the results from an online questionnaire completed by 246 respondents of different European nationalities, who all had a similar profile (well-educated and with a cosmopolitan outlook). The questionnaire covered five different product categories: cars, watches, perfume, chocolate and shoes.

The results of the test did not support the first hypothesis. On the contrary, they showed that exposure to retro brands did not evoke nostalgic and emotional associations, and that those associations did not encourage a clear preference for a retro brand. The second hypothesis was, however, confirmed.

In contrast to the results of the Orth–Gal research (also carried out in 2012), the Cattaneo–Guerini experiment suggested that nostalgic associations alone are not sufficient to make an old brand relevant for modern consumers. In this respect, Cattaneo and Guerini refined the conclusions reached by Orth and Gal, by pointing out that the updating of product characteristics is essential for the success of any retro branding strategy. Consumers are not motivated solely on the basis of associations to buy a retro brand rather than a newer alternative. In other words, nostalgia alone is not the core of a retro branding strategy. Instead, it is the specific product specifications – and, in particular, the new and innovative characteristics of the product – that encourages consumers to buy a retro brand in preference to a newer brand.

In short, retro brands need to be modernized so that consumers can regard them as being 'even better' than in the past. Launching an exact reproduction of the old product or service will not work, since that product or service will no longer meet today's more demanding standards and requirements. This explains why Heineken in The Netherlands uses nostalgic-looking labels on brand-new aluminum cans.

Updated characteristics are what inherently distinguish a retro brand from a nostalgic brand. Retro brands and retro products are brands and products that integrate old-fashioned design with modern functionality. They combine old and new, yesterday and today. This is the overall conclusion of the Cattaneo–Guerini research.

And there are numerous successful examples of this in practice. One of them is the legendary Fiat 500. This popular model from 1957 was re-launched exactly half a century later. Instead of introducing a completely new model, Fiat decided to build on the reputation of an iconic model from the past, while at the same time offering a 'new' car suited to all the requirements of modern city motoring. Or as the Fiat press release put it: 'We wanted to keep the proportions and identity of the car, but in a modern interpretation.'[12] The success of the car throughout Europe confirms the theory that the evoking of positive characteristics from the past, but without being an exact copy, is the key to a successful retro branding strategy. The balance between the retro-image of the car, with its iconic chrome door handles, and its state-of-the-art technology (Blue&Me, USB port, etc) created a total product that was a triumph.

Thoughts for the future

In addition to the Fiat 500, there are now numerous other examples, which prove that the retro branding strategy really works. Even so, a number of question marks remain. The current state of research does not allow any far-reaching conclusions to be drawn about the duration and effectiveness of this strategy in the long term. Orth and Gal were being admirably honest when they admitted that their 2012 study raised almost as many questions as it answered. Such as the question: can positively stimulated moods be maintained over a longer period by consumption or by memories?

Moreover, the current retro trend is taking place against a background of instability and crisis. This means that recent research has also been carried out in this same climate of economic malaise. There are various theories that see a clear connection between periods of crisis and a hankering for the happier days of the past. But no one has yet investigated whether nostalgia and retro branding strategies will still have the same major impact when the economic upturn begins. Will retro products and services still be as popular once the 'good times' return? Is retro branding just a temporary phenomenon?

It can also be asked whether a retro brand is distinctive enough today, in view of the large number of retro brands that have been launched on the market in recent years. It sometimes seems that retro branding strategies are being increasingly used as a tactic of last resort to make outdated brands relevant again.

Are the concerns implicit in these questions justified? Time will tell.

Summary

In turbulent times especially, people need reassurance and certainty. They become nostalgic and look to the past, when things were happier and more secure. This helps them to feel better.

The purchase behaviour of consumers can be influenced in part by the need to improve their mood and brands can positively stimulate this mood by evoking nostalgic memories. But nostalgia alone is not sufficient to motivate a consumer to make a purchase. Recent research has shown that the key to success lies in achieving a perfect balance between the old and the new: an old-fashioned design (which offers reassurance and certainty) combined with innovative characteristics (which satisfy modern requirements).

Brands must do more than simply confirm the consumer's perception that things were better in the past. They must also convince and inspire consumers, by proving that today's 'new' retro brand is better than yesterday's original.

Practical inspiration

1 Must a brand always look back to the past in uncertain times, so that it can appear solid and reliable to consumers?

2 Does the history of your brand have any possible significance for the advertising of the brand today?

3 What do you think about the idea of 'creating' a history for a brand?

4 What other methods can be used to make consumers believe that your brand is authentic?

5 Does a brand that positions itself on the basis of its past risk appearing old-fashioned to a new generation of consumers?

CASE STUDY   Procter & Gamble: Old Spice

Old Spice has been an icon in men's grooming since 1937. Today, in the advertising world, it has become an icon of an old brand that has been revived with a new, modern personality. With the launch of Axe, the brand's share had begun to deteriorate in the face of competition from this young, sex-driven challenger. As Old Spice had accumulated years and years of masculine experience, the brand decided to celebrate its heritage and reframe the 'old' into a relevant and compelling point-of-difference (separating the men from the boys). The brand's most iconic assets were recaptured and updated (for example, by replacing the original horse by a modern car and by featuring cult icon Bruce Campbell in the TV ads and in print). Since its re-launch, metrics illustrate the effectiveness of the campaign: brand relevance went up by 10 per cent and brand perception by 12 per cent. In 2011, there was a veritable award stampede (Grand Prix at Cannes, Grand North American Effie, Emmy for Outstanding Commercial, etc).

SOURCE Warc (2011). Old Spice: The Man Your Man Could Smell Like... Consulted online: www.warc.com

Notes

1   Carlin, G (1998) *Brain Droppings*, Hyperion, New York

2   Stern, B (1992) Historical and personal nostalgia in advertising text: the *fin-de-siècle* effect, *Journal of Advertising*, **31** (4), pp 11–22

3   Cattaneo, E and Guerini, C (2012) Assessing the revival potential of brands from the past: how relevant is nostalgia in retro branding strategies? *Journal of Brand Management*, **19** (8), pp 680–87

4   Jameson, F (1991) *Post-modernism, or the Cultural Logic of Late Capitalism*, Verso, London

5   See 2

6   Orth, U R and Gal, S (2012) Nostalgic brands as mood boosters, *Journal of Brand Management*, **19** (8), pp 666–79

7   Merchant, A *et al* (2013) How strong is the pull of the past? Measuring personal nostalgia evoked by advertising, *Journal of Advertising Research*, **53** (2), pp 150–65

8   See 3

9   Brown, S, Kozinets, R V and Sherry Jr, J F (2003) Teaching old brands new tricks: retro branding and the revival of brand meaning, *Journal of Marketing*, **67** (3), pp 19–33

10 See 3 and 8

11 Aaker, D A (1996) *Building Strong Brands*, Free Press, New York

12 See 3, 8 and 10

✤ PART THREE ✤
The reckoning

09

Advertising and ROI

Although much ink has already been spilt on the subject of the measurability and impact of advertising efforts, the discussion nevertheless remains an important one for today's marketers. In these difficult economic times and in an era of growing transparency, it is important for advertising – like all other commercial functions within a company – to show that it is paying its way. This need for accountability is hardly surprising, if you consider that in many companies marketing and advertising account for almost a third of the total budget.[1]

It is no secret that in times of economic recession the marketing function is one of the first to be re-examined more closely by the cost-cutting specialists. The days when marketers could defend their budgets with unfounded promises of increased sales, greater market shares, super-satisfied customers, etc, are long gone. Although some marketers look back wistfully on those easier times, the evolutions in terms of accountability present new opportunities for marketing to occupy a more strategic position in business operations. If marketing departments can show with hard facts and figures that they are contributing significantly to the (financial) success of the company, then the marketing profession will have taken an important step along the path to adulthood. The age of marketing puberty is in the past: financially, the time has come for marketing to stand on its own two feet.

What tools do advertisers have at their disposal to build up the financial case for advertising? What effect does advertising as a marketing instrument have on the company results? Is there any point in cutting back advertising effort and expenditure during periods of economic crisis? What importance do shareholders attach to advertising? These are questions that not only occupy the minds of marketers, but increasingly occupy the minds of financial directors and general managers as well.

ROMI: Measuring is knowing

To show that marketing and advertising really work, it is necessary to provide hard evidence. In this respect, measuring is knowing. It sounds simple. But to measure, you first need reliable measuring instruments – and that is where the problems start. There is no generally accepted, common measuring system for marketing. It is true that people juggle with terms like return on marketing investment (or ROMI), but there is no clear definition about what ROMI represents, nor is there any system to measure it. In theory, finding a system is not difficult; the real difficulty is that marketers cannot agree about what it should actually measure.[2]

In spite of much research, opinions about the best way to measure marketing return still vary widely. In fact, not everyone believes that marketing can be measured with a single system. Or as Charles Taylor of Villanova University expressed it in the *International Journal of Advertising*:[3] 'The weight of current evidence suggests that it is unlikely that a single measuring system can establish in an appropriate manner the results achieved by marketing.' However, Taylor also thinks that further research into the subject would be more than welcome.

Professor David W Stewart of the University of California brought together his ideas on the measuring of marketing return into a paper that was published in the *Journal of Advertising Research* in 2008. The first necessary step, according to Stewart, is to fix generally agreed standards. This immediately raises the central question: what should be measured? He argues that two separate aspects need to be assessed. Firstly, a list of the activities to be measured must be drawn up. After all, a sales conversation is not the same thing as a marketing commercial. In addition, it is necessary to assess the extent to which these activities contribute to the financial results of the company. The second aspect relates to the characteristics of the measuring itself: the data that are used must be both valid and reliable. On the basis of these starting points, Stewart then lists his own 12 'commandments' – or do's and don'ts – for an ideal measuring standard for ROMI.[4]

He argues that there must be a fundamental link between ROMI and financial performance. In concrete terms, this means that every item of marketing expenditure must be weighed against alternative (non-marketing-related) expenditure or against a scenario in which no expenditure is required. Consequently, the measuring of ROMI should be defined in terms of concepts such as return, risk, the time value of money and the cost of capital. The measuring must be able to estimate the risks attached to marketing actions and to adjust the ROI in function of those risks.

Moreover, not only the results of implemented marketing actions need to be measured. Measuring must also have a predictive function. It should take into account both short-term and long-term effects and should be finely-meshed enough to indicate when certain actions over a period of time are either profitable or unprofitable.

In today's marketing world, most measurements deal with matters such as effort (reach, frequency, etc), efficiency (eg, cost per contact) or productivity (eg, average cost per sale). According to Stewart, a good measuring of ROMI should focus first and foremost on results, in combination with efficiency and productivity, and with a clear link to financial performance. ROMI needs to be measured in this manner, so that the information is comparable for different products, markets and companies, but also to take into account the fact that some products and markets yield a different return. Finally, the correct measuring of the return on marketing activities must be seen as a strategic instrument that helps companies to improve their accountability, operational effectiveness, reputation and transparency when making decisions. The only question that remains to be answered is this: who will take the initiative to create such a measuring standard? In general, there are three ways to achieve this. Firstly, the government can impose a standard. Secondly, the sectorial organizations can join forces to agree on a standard. Thirdly, a standard can be developed as a result of competition in the market place. Stewart believes that the third option is the most realistic one, and he hopes that his guidelines can be a useful point of reference for future efforts in this direction.

The fact that there is currently no agreed standard measuring instrument for marketing clearly works to the disadvantage of the marketers. How can they prove that marketing has a positive effect? In the context of the difficulties of the current economic situation, how can they show the potential long-term benefits of marketing activities? Or is expenditure on marketing simply a short-term cost?

The value of a company is made up of tangible and intangible assets. Stewart argues that the added value of marketing is also tangible and intangible. The tangible added value of marketing is expressed in increased sales and profit. The less (or non-) tangible benefits include better brand equity and increased publicity. All this suggests that in addition to direct effects (on sales and profits), advertising also has an indirect impact on the overall worth of the company.[5]

'ROMI must focus on results, efficiency, productivity and financial performance.'

FIGURE 9.1   Commercial and financial effects of advertising

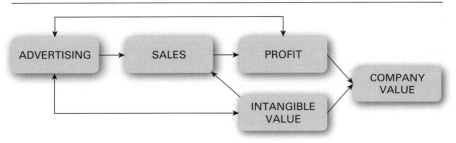

Advertising has a double effect. It generates greater sales of products and services, which leads to greater profitability and a higher company value. Advertising also contributes to the building up of strong brand equity, which can also be translated into financial value as part of the overall value of the company.

(Source: adapted from Stewart, How marketing contributes to the bottom line, *Journal of Advertising Research*, 2008)

Advertising in times of recession

Traditionally, the effect of advertising is linked to an increase in sales and the profitability of the company. For this reason, most research into the impact of advertising focuses on these 'indirect' effects: advertising as a means to convince consumers to purchase products and services, which in turn leads to bigger profits. Indirect effects of this kind are often measured in terms of advertising elasticity. This is the percentage increase in sales as a result of an increase in advertising expenditure of 1 per cent.

In a recent meta-analytical investigation, Raj Sethuraman, Gerard J Tellis and Richard Briesch examined no fewer than 56 research studies about advertising elasticity, published between 1960 and 2008. They looked at both the short-term and long-term effects for consumer brands in different categories. The results were published in the *Journal of Marketing Research* and were compared by the authors with the results of a similar project carried out in 1984.[6] What did this comparison reveal? Today's average advertising elasticity in the short term is 0.12, which is just half of the comparable figure from 1984 (0.22). The same trend is also evident for long-term advertising elasticity, where the average figure has fallen from 0.41 to 0.22 since 1984. The good news for European brands is that their average advertising elasticity of 0.17 is significantly higher than the 0.11 of the United States. It is possible that there is a degree of under-advertising in Europe, as a result of legislative restrictions, while at the same time there is probably a degree of over-advertising in the less regulated United States.

The recent study also allows a more nuanced picture to be painted. For example, it revealed that advertising elasticity is higher for durables than for non-durables. Typical examples of durables are cars, household appliances and electronic equipment. It also showed that advertising elasticity is higher during the earlier phases of the product life cycle than in the later phases. Once again, this is particularly true for durables, which proves the value of advertising for the launching of new products. Similarly, advertising elasticity is higher over a period of a year than over a single quarter, which demonstrates that advertising primarily generates positive effects over a longer period. Perhaps most significantly – and contrary to what is often supposed – advertising elasticity does not decline during periods of recession. In fact, its level remains static or even increases. In view of this, the authors strongly recommend in their conclusions that companies should not cut their advertising budgets during periods of economic downturn.

This is a key point for advertising agencies and advertisers alike, since they are often the first to feel the effects when the economic storm clouds begin to gather. But is this right? Should companies cut advertising expenditure in times of crisis? Or should they actually be increasing it? Professor Gerard J Tellis decided to look into this important matter and in 2009 published the results of his study of existing empirical research in the *Journal of Advertising Research*. Tellis analysed 10 reports compiled between 1920 and 2005, the majority in respect of US companies. It was possible to divide the reports into two broad themes: the effect of economic cycles on advertising in general and the effect of advertising by individual companies on their sales, market share and profitability.[7]

One of the large international studies investigated by Tellis confirmed that advertising in the different major economies of the world is (as already suggested above) subject to the fluctuations of economic cycles. It concluded that a positive or negative change of 1 per cent in gross domestic product (GDP) will be accompanied by a change of 1.4 per cent in advertising expenditure in the same direction. This cyclic effect is felt more strongly in countries where the focus is more on the short term than on the long term. According to this researcher, advertisements in the written press are also more susceptible to economic change than TV commercials. But in the context of 'advertising and ROI', it is also interesting to note that two of the other studies argued that house brands or private labels actually behave in an anti-cyclical manner. This means that in comparison with general brands, they do better when the economy shrinks. Moreover, their increase in market share in times of recession is greater than the decrease they experience during periods of economic growth. Better still, a number of these private labels are even able to retain their increase once the recession comes to an end.

As far as the effect of advertising on sales is concerned, the majority of the empirical reports analysed by Tellis concluded that the cutting of advertising budgets in times of recession can have a negative effect on sales, both during and after the recession, without resulting in any significant additional profit. Companies that invested more in advertising during periods of recession saw their sales, market share and profitability all rise, once again both during and after the recession. A number of the studies also showed that the positive effects of the advertising strategy adopted during the recession were still being felt several years later.

With regard to the impact of advertising on profitability, the results of the various studies were not wholly consistent. Two of the studies concluded that there can be no question of increased profits when advertising budgets are cut during periods of recession. According to a third study, the mainte-nance of advertising budgets leads to a growth in net income, while the increase of advertising efforts during a recession leads to greater revenues than would otherwise be the case if the same efforts were made during a period of economic growth. However, two other studies concluded that spending more on advertising during a recession does not lead to a bigger return on investment.

'Cutting advertising budgets in times of recession can have a negative effect on sales, both during and after the recession.'

The different studies investigated by Tellis highlight the various advantages and disadvantages of cutting, maintaining or increasing advertising efforts during a recession. According to Tellis, the main argument in favour of cutting budgets during difficult economic conjunctures is to 'optimize' these budgets, by bringing them back into line with the reduced level of sales that can be expected during the downturn. The strongest argument in favour of advertising more during a recession is that companies can advertise more effectively, because there is less competition from other advertising campaigns. If less people are advertising, your campaign is more likely to stand out. Tellis also points out that the research studies to date make no distinction between strong companies and weak companies. He suggests that it is perfectly possible that stronger companies will be more inclined to invest in advertising during a recession, whereas their weaker counterparts will be more likely to cut advertising budgets during difficult periods.

To some extent, Tellis's findings have been confirmed by subsequent research carried out by Jan-Benedict Steenkamp and Eric Fang, the results of which were published in *Marketing Science* in 2011.[8] Their study covered 1,175 US companies over a period of three decades. They concluded that increasing advertising share of voice during a period of recession has a stronger influence on profits and market share than when levels of advertising are increased during a period of economic expansion. However, their results also show that the effectiveness of advertising is dependent upon the cyclicity of the sector. For example, the effect of advertising in a strongly cyclic sector can be 50 per cent greater in terms of market share and 200 per cent greater in terms of profit, when compared with a sector with average cyclicity. Moreover, this 'cyclicity factor' – which indicates the impact of the conjuncture – seems to manifest itself most frequently and most forcefully during periods of recession.

Another recent research study indicates that the effect of advertising during economic downturns is above all dependent upon the financial leverage of the advertising company. Financial leverage is the extent to which a company can finance its activities through borrowing. The greater the company's financial leverage, the greater the increase in profitability resulting from additional advertising during a recession becomes.[9]

There are dozens of old and new examples of companies which, in spite of everything, continued to invest in advertising during difficult economic times. Procter & Gamble has long been the world's biggest advertiser. They even increased their advertising efforts during the Great Depression of the 1930s, in part to launch their 'Ivory' soap brand onto the market. More recent examples included microchip manufacturer Intel, which launched its massive *Intel Inside* campaign during the economic slump at the beginning of the 1990s. Yet, although the major advertisers like Procter & Gamble and Unilever have maintained or increased their worldwide advertising activities during the past decade, there has recently been a noticeable decline in the number of advertising commissions in Europe: an almost 4 per cent decrease between the second quarter of 2011 and the second quarter of 2012.[10] Europe is the only region in the world where this trend is evident – which is no doubt connected with the persistence of the current economic and financial crisis.

Do investors like advertising?

Empirical research has therefore shown that advertising can be linked to better financial performance and that in times of recession it can even lead to better sales results, a bigger share of market and increased profitability. These are the direct effects of advertising. But does advertising also have an indirect effect on the financial markets? Does it influence the evaluations that investors make of companies and shares?

An event study of the relationship between the notorious Super Bowl advertising and advertisers' market valuation showed that Super Bowl advertising indeed results in an average of 0.8 per cent increase in advertisers' stock prices.[11]

Hence, nowadays, management decisions are taken increasingly on the basis of the likely added value they can give to shareholders. This applies as much to marketing as it does to human resources or production. For shareholders, the price of the share or the market cap are their yardsticks for measuring success. This, at least, is the opinion of Professors Amit Joshi of the University of Central Florida and Dominique Hanssens of the UCLA Anderson School of Management, whose research study into the effect of advertising on stock market prices was published in the *Journal of Marketing* in 2010.[12]

It is no secret that marketers often struggle with the problem of justifying their actions. They have equal difficulty in persuading people of the positive effects of their expenditure. As a result, they are often judged by the financial management of the company over the short term, on the basis of sales figures and profits. According to Joshi and Hanssens, the principle of shareholder value analysis (SVA) offers marketers the chance to show the value of their marketing efforts over the long term, in a manner that demonstrates their real added value to shareholders. This is not straightforward, since marketing value (as previously mentioned) consists of both tangible and non-tangible elements, which often adds to the pressure on marketing and advertising budgets.

The researchers hypothesized that advertising not only has an impact in the short term, but also has a positive effect over a longer period, in terms of the return on the company's shares. They see two possible reasons for this. The first is the so-called 'spillover effect'. This means that investors have a preference for strong and well-known brands, because they think that brand awareness and a good perception of brand quality will have an influence – a 'spillover' – on demand for the shares of the companies with these strong brands in their portfolio. The second possible reason is the signalling effect. This means that investment in advertising is interpreted by investors as a sign of the good financial health of the company in question.

Joshi and Hanssens tested their hypotheses against the performance of some of the leading companies in the United States: the computer manufacturers Apple, Compaq, Dell, HP and IBM and the manufacturers of sports articles Nike, Reebok, K-Swiss and Sketchers. Together these companies represent a significant portion of their respective industries. Data was collected for a lengthy period: 10 years for the sportswear manufacturers and 15 years for the computer manufacturers. The material analysed included turnover figures, income, share return, advertising expenditure, R&D expenditure and innovation announcements.

The research showed that a change in advertising expenditure is not reflected in the immediate short term in a change in the stock market price of the company's shares. This is not surprising. The stock market and the investors are not directly informed by the company of an increase in the advertising budget. They only become aware of this when they later come into contact with the resulting advertising campaign. The effect is therefore a long-term one. In this respect, the results of the research confirmed the Joshi–Hanssens hypotheses to a large extent. Apple, Compaq, Dell and HP all saw a significant and positive response from investors. At IBM the response was positive, but not significant – which the researchers attributed to the fact that the computer activities of IBM only represent 11 per cent of their total turnover. As far as the manufacturers of sports articles were concerned, there was a significant effect in three of the four companies, with the largest effect being seen at the youngest of the three: Sketchers.

A further important conclusion from the study was that – in the case of Dell, HP, Nike and Reebok – advertising also had a positive effect on share value, without there being any corresponding and measurable effect in terms of sales. However, the opposite effect was noted for IBM and K-Swiss, where advertising had an effect on consumers, but not on investors. This latter effect was a general one: advertising has less impact on investors than on consumers – which is also logical, since investors are not the primary target of advertising. On the benefits side, advertising has a double effect in the financial field. Not only does it have a positive effect on the company's own share value, but it can also have a negative effect on the share value of other sectoral competitors that have a comparable market value.

Does this all mean that unlimited investment in advertising can lead to unlimited growth on the stock market? No. The results of the research showed that the financial markets punish companies where the level of advertising varies markedly (in either positive or negative terms) from what is regarded as the 'optimum' level. Consequently, the impact of an increase in advertising expenditure on the stock market value of companies can be important, but only within the limits of what is economically reasonable.

Advertising or R&D?

That investors are sensitive to advertising expenditure in times of economic crisis was also evident from the study conducted by Professor Surinder Tikoo of the State University of New York and Dr Ahmed Ebrahim of Fairfield University, the results of which were published in the *Journal of Advertising Research* in 2010. Their investigations focused on the reactions of the financial markets to additional expenditure or savings in R&D and advertising during the recession.[13]

Investors attach great importance, not least in times of recession, to the previously mentioned items of 'discretionary' expenditure; in other words, items of expenditure about which there is a choice whether or not to incur them.

Advertising and R&D are two of the most important items of discretionary expenditure. Both can make significant contributions towards future earnings potential by creating or supporting a number of the company's intangible assets. Advertising, for example, can help to build up the strength of a brand, which can generate different competitive advantages, including premium pricing. In the long term, this can have a positive influence on sales.

During times of crisis, companies react in different ways to discretionary expenditure. Some decide to increase their advertising budgets; others prefer to cut them. Investors also react differently during periods of economic malaise. They generally have a preference for low-risk activities that offer a return in the short term. Research has shown that investment in R&D is regarded as being more risky than investment in advertising, primarily because R&D requires a larger initial investment and its possible benefits are often only seen much further down the line.

For their study, Tikoo and Ebrahim looked at the evolution of US shares during the recession period 2000 to 2002. They came to the conclusion that investors reacted more favourably to companies that boosted their investment in advertising, as opposed to companies that devoted extra financial resources to R&D. The financial markets regard a stronger focus on advertising and a weaker focus on R&D as the best strategy to maintain revenue levels during difficult economic times.

These findings do nothing to detract from the necessity for companies and brands to continue investing in innovation as a blueprint for future success. Innovations (particularly in the form of brand extensions) are the oxygen for brands that want to survive.

Strong brands have added financial value

In 2002, Professors Thomas J Madden and Susan M Fournier, together with financial expert Frank Fehle, carried out a research study to establish the link between the activities – such as advertising – that companies initiate to build up their brands and the added value to shareholders.[14] Previous research had already demonstrated that a positive relationship exists between brand equity and the share price. But do companies that invest in their brand perform better on the stock market? That is what Madden, Fournier and Fehle wanted to find out.

They examined the financial performance between 1994 and 2001 of the most valued brands, as listed by Interbrand. This was then compared with the financial performance of companies that made less strenuous efforts to build up their brand(s). The results showed that the strong brands performed significantly better on the stock market during this period. Moreover, the additional revenues from branding did not involve a higher degree of company risk. This indicated that investment in branding not only provides extra income for brands in development, but also for established brands.

On the basis of these results, the research team argues that the impact of marketing efforts on the financial results of the company should also be included in the company's financial reporting. They also point to the possible role that brands, brand extensions and brand management can play in the financial risk management of companies. A brand is typically described as an asset to which a value must be ascribed or even as a cost that needs to be controlled, but seldom, if ever, as an instrument for risk management. But if the performance of a brand has a direct impact on the financial results of a company, this implies that better or worse management of the brand will also have respectively a positive or negative influence on the financial risks that the company runs.

Summary

Advertising elasticity continues to be important, but less so than in the past. Nevertheless, research has shown that the brands that increase advertising expenditure in times of crisis benefit from higher sales figures, a larger share of market and increased profitability. These effects are lasting over a long period, even when the economy recovers. If an average brand maintains or increases advertising expenditure during a recession, this will lead to a greater increase in profits than if the brand maintains or increases advertising expenditure during non-recession periods.

Advertising also has a positive long-term effect on the share return of a company. In times of recession, brands that invest more in advertising (and less in R&D) have a greater beneficial impact on the stock market price of their shares than brands that invest more in R&D (and less in advertising). Advertising therefore has a positive effect on the financial markets.

Practical inspiration

1 Calculate the advertising elasticity of your brand over a period of one to two years. What was the effect on sales or market share?

2 Analyse the advertising expenditure of different brands within a certain category over the period 2008–2013 and discuss the resulting changes in market share.

3 How did the advertising expenditure of your company evolve during the period 2008–2012? What arguments were used to justify these evolutions?

4 What criteria do you use to measure the ROI of your brand? Evaluate the ROI over a longer period.

5 When you are planning advertising campaigns, do you take into account the possible positive impact on the stock market value of your company?

CASE STUDY The Mercedes Benz 'C Class' Coupé

This Mercedes case illustrates that investing in marketing and advertising in economic troubled times can definitely result in growth, even in one of the most difficult and shrinking markets like automotive. The launch of the 'C-Class' Coupé – completely new model – heralded in a new era for Mercedes Benz. The company hoped to break with the traditional 'classic' image of the C Class, so that it could recapture consumers who in recent years had moved away to the trendier Audi and BMW brands. In 2012, Mercedes Benz in Germany underwent a transformation: suddenly it was seen as younger, spontaneous and trend-setting. This was reflected in the sales figures: these rose by 43 points in the month following the campaign. In recognition of the campaign's excellence and effectiveness, it was awarded a silver Euro Effie in 2012.

SOURCE Euro Effie Awards (2012). Mercedes. Venice/C-Class Coupé. Consulted online: http://www.adforum.com/euro-effie/2012/

Notes

1 Stewart, D W (2008) How marketing contributes to the bottom line, *Journal of Advertising Research*, **48** (1), pp 94–105

2 See 1

3 Taylor, C R (2010) Measuring return on investment from advertising: 'Holy Grail' or necessary tool? *International Journal of Advertising*, **29** (3), pp 345–48

4 See 1 and 2

5 Joshi, A and Hanssens, D M (2010) The direct and indirect effects of advertising on firm value, *Journal of Marketing*, **74** (1), pp 20–33

6 Sethuraman, R, Tellis, G J and Briesch, R A (2011) How well does advertising work? Generalizations from meta-analysis of brand advertising elasticities, *Journal of Marketing Research*, **48** (3), pp 457–71

7 Tellis, G J and Tellis, K (2009) A critical review and synthesis of research on advertising in a recession, *Journal of Advertising Research*, **49** (3), pp 304–27

8 Steenkamp, J B E M and Fang, E (2011) The impact of economic contractions on the effectiveness of R&D and advertising: evidence from US companies spanning three decades, *Marketing Science*, **30** (4), pp 628–45

9 Srinivasan, R, Lilien, G L and Sridhar, S (2011) Should firms spend more on research and development and advertising during recessions? *Journal of Marketing*, **75** (3), pp 49–65

10 Nielsen Report [accessed 19 September 2012] Global Adview Pulse, Q2 2012 [Online] http://www.nielsen.com/us/en/reports/2012/global-adview-pulse-lite--q2-2012.html

11 Kim, J W, Freling, T H and Grisaffe, D B (2013) The secret sauce for Super Bowl advertising: what makes marketing work in the world's most watched event? *Journal of Advertising Research*, **53** (2), pp 134–49

12 See 5

13 Tikoo, S and Ebrahim, A (2010) Financial markets and marketing: the tradeoff between R&D and advertising during an economic downturn, *Journal of Advertising Research*, **50** (1), pp 50–56

14 Madden, T J, Fehle, F and Fournier, S M (2006) Brands matter: an empirical investigation of brand-building activities and the creation of shareholder value, *Journal of the Academy of Marketing Science*, **34** (2), pp 224–35

10

The new capitalism

Consumers are turning their backs on advertising, or so it is said, because it is no longer 'trustworthy' or 'credible'. The call for regulation, self-regulation and a more ethical approach in marketing and advertising is getting louder and louder. But at the same time we need to ask ourselves whether or not we can imagine a world without advertising. What lessons can marketers and advertisers draw from all this criticism? In this final chapter, the importance of ethics in advertising and the need for a new form of capitalism will be discussed.

The debate about the impact of advertising on our daily lives and culture has been going on for some time and has become even more intense in recent years. This is no surprise. The current financial and economic crisis has not only shaken the financial system to its very foundations, but has also inspired a wider debate about the way in which capitalism and our consumption-based society seem more inclined to destroy than to help us achieve prosperity and well-being. Some people regard advertising as being one of the main causes of this sorry situation. In their eyes, advertising creates needs that drive the consumption behaviour that is so harmful to society. Not only because consumption continues to eat into our scarce natural resources, but also because advertising undermines our cultural values.

Are these criticisms of advertising justified? Should advertisers and the advertisement makers be looking to find a new direction? Or is advertising as good as dead?

Mirror, mirror on the wall. . .

The ethical debate surrounding advertising was brought into sharp focus by the report published in 2011 by the British section of the World Wildlife Fund (WWF), in collaboration with the British Public Interest Research Centre (PIRC). Under the evocative title 'Think of me as evil? Opening the ethical debate in advertising', the report turned the harsh spotlight of public opinion on the advertising industry. Although the authors admitted that the research on which they based their findings did not always provide sufficient or conclusive evidence, the report was not very positive in its assessment of advertising and advertisers – and that's putting it mildly![1]

The report attempted to answer three fundamental ethical questions. The first of these questions asked whether advertising actually makes people consume more by continually creating new needs. In other words, does advertising help to grow the consumer market in its totality or does it only ensure that existing levels of consumption are redistributed between the different players in the market? According to the authors, the various academic and scientific studies on this subject do not conclusively prove the matter one way or the other, but 'it seems that advertising encourages society to save less, borrow more, work harder and consume larger quantities of material goods'. One of the most well-known and emotive examples linked to this conclusion is tobacco advertising. The report pointed out that a recent meta-study carried out by the United States Department of Health established that there was a causal connection between tobacco advertising/promotion and the use of tobacco. It also seemed likely, the WWF/PIRC report continued, 'that tobacco advertising not only redistributes consumption between the different brands, but also increases the overall size of the market'.

The second question asked by the report is whether advertising is simply a reflection of society and its values, or whether it also strengthens and 'normalizes' the values it projects. And in view of the fact that advertising is ever present in all our lives, does it actually influence our values? The researchers used, as their starting point, a psychological model, which contends that people allow themselves (and their behaviour) to be shaped by intrinsic and extrinsic values. Intrinsic values are related to the things that we strive for because they are valuable or worthwhile in themselves, such as a sense of community, self-development or the companionship of family and friends. Extrinsic values are related to the perceptions of others, such as conformity, image, power and material success. The authors claim that advertising focuses on extrinsic values, which in turn are associated with lower levels of motivation to tackle social and environmental problems. In cases where advertising does appeal to intrinsic values, this – according to the report – does more harm than good, because it creates the perception that intrinsic values can be achieved through the purchase of particular products. When a product does not live up to this expectation, this can weaken people's resolve to strive for intrinsic values at all. To make matters worse – again according to the report – advertising does indeed strengthen the values that it seeks to exploit. And if these values are primarily extrinsic, advertising will therefore ensure that people who are exposed to such values become more attached to them, at the expense of more socially responsible values and the environment. Furthermore, conclude the authors, the influence of advertising on cultural values is unrelated to the product being advertised and its purchase. In other words, a green car being promoted by a glamorous movie star probably does more to emphasize extrinsic values (status and social comparison) than intrinsic ones (concern for the environment). Trying to publicize environmental problems by advertising that appeals to extrinsic values is 'like poisoning the roots of the tree while you are watering its leaves'.

The third question asked is whether advertising increases the consumer's freedom of choice or actually limits it. The report contends that advertising works in part through an unconscious response in the consumer's brain, which is more likely to restrict choice than broaden it. When we 'process' advertising unconsciously, we are less aware of the influence that the advertisement is having on us. The argument that people should be better 'educated' to deal with media and advertising does not hold water, say the authors, since even people who are 'media-aware' are not immune to the unconscious influences to which they are being subjected. For this reason, the authors are concerned in particular about the influence of advertising on children, since they are even more susceptible. The choice of the consumer is even further restricted by the fact that advertising is increasingly ever present in our lives. Freedom of choice, concludes the report, must not only be limited to freedom of commercial choice between different brands, but must include the choice not to be exposed to advertising.

The WWF/PIRC report is tough on the advertising industry. The authors claim that their purpose was to encourage the sector to look at itself more closely in the mirror and to show – if it can – that the net impact of advertising is positive. With this aim in mind, the report makes a number of recommendations:

Firstly, it argues that the influence of advertising on cultural values must be reduced. This means that companies must look critically at the values they appeal to in their advertising campaigns. NGOs and other social organizations must increase the pressure on the advertising world to turn its back on advertising that places too strong an emphasis on extrinsic values. In this respect, there is a need for further research and appropriate legislation.

Secondly, the report suggests that the sheer quantity of advertising and its ubiquity need to be addressed. The basic premise of the authors is that we should move towards a world in which people are free to choose whether they are exposed to advertising or not. This means that 'opt-out' possibilities need to be strengthened; that advertising aimed at children should be restricted; and that alternative financial models should be explored for news and leisure activities.

The WWF/PIRC report claims that research shows that the public is becoming increasingly irritated by advertising that seems to be omnipresent. Figures from the Digital Advertising Attitudes Report for 2012 by Upstream and YouGov confirm that the saturation point for digital marketing is rapidly being reached. Two-thirds of the British and US consumers questioned said that they saw too many online adverts and received too many online promo-offers. Many of them are fed up with this constant bombardment. More than one in four Brits and one in five Americans said that they would turn against any brand that continued to irritate them too frequently with unsolicited digital advertising or promotions.[2]

The criticism of advertising contained in the WWF/PIRC report boils down to two main charges. On the one hand, the ethics of advertising practice are challenged. On the other hand, the consumer society and the capitalist model on which it is based are called into question. These are complex issues, which no doubt explains why they have been the subjects of heated discussion for many years. Nevertheless, new voices are now being heard in both the advertising industry and in the world of business; voices that are developing some interesting solutions to these crucial problems.

Ethical advertising as the norm

Many marketers and advertisers are well aware that there is still much work to be done in the field of ethical advertising. They are equally aware that there is much at stake. In 2011, the *Journal of Advertising Research* devoted the whole of its September edition to advertising ethics. In the foreword, marketing professor Richard Beltramini from Wayne State University said that there are still many unanswered questions about advertising's informative and persuasive role. He argues that the time has come to make a major effort to move beyond the often-hollow ethical codes that are currently in use. The first step is to focus much more on the issues involved. In future, academics and advertisers will need to work together more closely and must launch new initiatives, such as the organization of national ethical conferences, at which recognized authorities in ethical matters will talk on key subjects.[3]

In the same September edition, Wally Snyder, director of the American Institute for Advertising Ethics, defended the case for an improved form of ethics in advertising. According to Snyder, companies can only benefit from adopting a more ethical approach to their advertising practices.[4] Firstly, because customers place a high value on ethical companies and are even prepared to pay more for ethically manufactured products – as was made clear by a study published in the *Wall Street Journal* in 2008. The impact that advertising can have on the ethical image of a company was demonstrated in another research study carried out by students from the Missouri School of Journalism in 2009. 'Honest advertising' was indicated by the respondents as being the most important factor (89 per cent) in determining whether or not a company is perceived as ethical by consumers, followed by 'a sense of social responsibility' (80 per cent) and 'environmental friendliness' (59 per cent).

Snyder argues that marketers need to become (or be made) more aware of the fact that ethical and honest advertising make a major contribution to the way customers view the ethical image of a company. And advertisers must also recognize – and accept – that today's consumers often feel that they are being sold short in terms of honest advertising. Research by *Adweek* Media/Harris Poll in 2010 revealed that only one American in five 'usually believes advertising'; whereas 13 per cent said that they 'never believe advertising'. It is the large, middle group of 65 per cent, the group which says that they 'sometimes believe advertising', which offers most potential as a target public for more ethical advertising.

According to Snyder, advertising agencies and advertising professionals have a crucial role to play in helping to build up confidence in companies and brands. Ethics must be at the forefront of their thinking at all times. There must be clear guidelines and they must be enforced. Moreover, the ethical approach needs to permeate all levels of the sector, from general and commercial management to strategy, creation and production. Advertising professionals must be proactive in their dealings with ethical matters. Room must be created for internal discussion about advertising ethics, and any obstacles to talking about ethical problems must be removed.

It is not sufficient, continues Snyder, for advertising professionals simply to say that 'ethics are important' and that they are 'looking into the matter'. Nor is it enough for the managers of advertising bureaus to say 'I have told my people that they need to be ethical'. Leaders in the world of advertising must demonstrate the desire to run their businesses with staff who strive to achieve the very highest ethical standards, so that trust, loyalty and value can be created for the companies for which they work.

The EU Pledge

In December 2007, the EU Pledge was launched. This is a voluntary initiative by leading food and beverage companies to change food and beverage advertising to children under the age of 12 in the European Union.

The EU Pledge was part of signatories' commitment to the European Union Platform for Action on Diet, Physical Activity and Health, which is the multi-stakeholder forum set up by former EU Health and Consumer Affairs Commissioner Markos Kyprianou in 2005 to encourage stakeholders to promote healthy lifestyles in Europe. In the context of the EU Platform, the EU Pledge commitment is owned by the World Federation of Advertisers (WFA), which also supports the programme.

Companies that subscribe to the EU Pledge make the following commitments:

1 No advertising for food and beverage products to children under the age of 12 on TV, in print and on the internet, except for products which fulfil specific nutritional criteria based on accepted scientific evidence and/or applicable national and international dietary guidelines.

2 No communication related to products in primary schools, except where specifically requested by, or agreed with, the school administration for educational purposes.

EU Pledge member companies represent over three-quarters of food and beverage advertising expenditure in the EU. The initiative is open to any food and beverage company active in Europe and willing to subscribe to the EU Pledge commitments.

SOURCE The EU Pledge http://www.eu-pledge.eu

The new capitalism

Snyder pointed out that consumers reward the brands they perceive as ethical. But the ethical debate is not just about advertising. In fact, the debate encompasses the wider role of companies within the capitalist system. Advertising is just one way to roll out a company strategy and philosophy, by means of external communication relating to a brand or product. Many companies have now understood that ethics need to begin with a specific vision of entrepreneurship, including the role of companies in society and the manner in which they create value.

Harvard professor Michael Porter and CSR specialist Mark Kramer offered a ground-breaking vision of value creation in their article *Creating Shared Value*, which won the 2011 McKinsey Award for the most influential article of the year in the *Harvard Business Review*. The authors recognize that capitalism is currently under heavy fire, in particular because of its role in relation to serious social, environmental and economic problems. There is now a huge gap separating society at large and the business community – and it is up to the companies to bridge that gap.[5]

The Porter–Kramer solution goes beyond the classic definition of corporate social responsibility. Companies, they say, need to think about a new form of capitalism. In the 'old', existing form of capitalism, companies contribute to society by making profit. In this way, they also generate employment, wages, purchases, investments and taxes. As a result, they do not need to be overly concerned with social concerns and problems, which may actually get in the way of making profit. Porter and Kramer argue that it is possible to have a new form of capitalism; one which will allow this discredited economic model to renew its legitimization with society, leading to a new worldwide wave of innovation, productivity and growth. The answer is to be found in the principle of 'shared value': the creation of economic value in a manner that also creates value for society, by meeting its needs and providing solutions for its problems. The reasons for a company's existence must be redefined in terms of the creation of shared value. Multinationals like GE, Google, IBM, Intel, Johnson & Johnson, Nestlé, Unilever and Walmart have all made major efforts to develop new forms of value creation. If it is to be successful, this change of course requires a new type of leadership in companies, but also a new approach from governments.

According to Porter and Kramer, there are three ways a company can create shared value. The first is to re-evaluate their products and markets, so that they can better cater to the real needs of society. Companies sometimes forget to ask the simple question: is our product right for our customers or for the customers of our customers? Fortunately, there is a growing number of companies who do ask this question. For example, the US technology giant GE developed an innovative range of new products and services (no fewer than 140 by 2011) under the name 'Ecomagination'. Their stated aim was to 'tackle today's environmental problems, whilst at the same time creating economic growth'. And it seems to be working. Since its inception, the 'Ecomagination' range has generated $105 billion of turnover, far exceeding the company's own growth objectives. In fact, 'Ecomagination' is growing much faster than the rest of GE.

The second way for companies to create shared value is to redefine productivity in the value chain. The value chains of companies are closely linked to important societal challenges, such as the use of natural resources and water, health and safety, transport and distribution, working conditions and diversity. By rethinking the value chain, it is often possible for a company to reduce the burden of its operations on society and cut costs at the same time. For example, the British department store Marks & Spencer completely remodelled it logistics chain. The aim was to save £175 million by 2016, while at the same time drastically cutting its CO_2 emissions. Similarly, Coca-Cola has invested heavily in reducing its water use worldwide. In comparison with 2004, the company has improved its water efficiency by 20 per cent, and it has already set new objectives for 2020.

At the end of the 20th century, the Belgian company Umicore had a terrible record in environmental matters. But during the last decade the materials technology group has undergone a total transformation. This once-despised polluter now manufactures (amongst other things) catalytic converters that actually reduce car pollution and it has also become a leading specialist in recycling technology. These efforts have borne fruit. Almost 100 per cent of the noble metals used by the company are now obtained via recycling and in 2012 Umicore was high on the list of the world's most sustainable companies, according to the ranking compiled by the Canadian research agency, Corporate Knights. In a similar manner, iTunes and Kindle have shown that new distribution models can significantly reduce the use of plastic and paper.

Under the 'old' capitalist vision, the welfare of the workforce often had to take second place to productivity. But the concept of shared value can be applied here as well. Several pioneering companies have realized that investing in the health and well-being of staff also increases efficiency, not least through reduced sickness absence. This, at least, is the conclusion of Johnson & Johnson's worldwide healthcare programme.

The third and final element in Porter and Kramer's recipe for shared value is the development of local clusters or ecosystems. The success of a modern company is determined in part by its surrounding infrastructure and the network of organizations and institutions that supports it, such as universities, research centres, government authorities, etc. Companies can create shared value by setting up such clusters and tackling the problems that arise within the surrounding framework. Nestlé is an example of a company that has built up a network of clusters for its Nespresso brand, not only to improve the local production process, but also (in collaboration with an NGO) to encourage better and more sustainable agricultural practices.

Porter and Kramer are convinced that the idea of creating shared value is not an illusion. Profit made on the basis of meeting a societal need is, according to them, simply a higher form of capitalism, which should not be compared with charity or philanthropy. It is a new model that allows both societies and business to flourish alongside each other in a positive and sustainable spiral of growth. And the best opportunities to create shared value are to be found in the specific activities of the companies themselves.

'Creating shared value is not an illusion'

If every company is prepared to adopt the shared value principle, conclude Porter and Kramer, then society cannot fail to reap its share of the benefits. And although it may not be possible to solve all the many problems facing the world today, it would at least allow companies to utilize their strengths in the interests of social progress, while at the same time re-legitimizing their activities in the eyes of a public that has been increasingly sceptical in recent years.

The British-Dutch multinational Unilever is another example of a company that has understood this message. Unilever has developed a highly ambitious plan that seeks to reduce its ecological footprint by half before the year 2020. In this way, the company (best known for its popular consumer brands, like Bertolli, Dove and Axe) hopes to cut its water use, greenhouse gas emissions and packaging waste by 50 per cent. The aim is to provide much-needed drinking water to half a billion people around the planet. But this is not pure altruism. Unilever expects to see its revenue flow double by the end of the decade.

But the story doesn't end there. Shortly after his appointment in 2009, CEO Paul Polman scrapped all quarterly reports. In doing so, he wanted to shift the company's focus from the short term to the medium-long term. In an interview with the *Harvard Business Review*, he said that a company does not exist simply to satisfy its shareholders. According to Polman, this is a shortsighted attitude that thinks first and foremost of creating shareholder value, almost at the expense of everything else. What's more, it is an attitude that can boomerang with disastrous consequences in the medium to long term. When asked if he thought there was a risk that his alternative approach might drive away shareholders and investors, Polman turned the argument on its head: he believes that companies should attract shareholders who also believe in a long-term strategy, and not the other way around. His message for hedge funds and short-term speculators is unequivocal: 'You don't belong in our company. Just because you buy a few shares, it doesn't give you the right to turn our strategy upside down.' In other words, they are free to go somewhere else.[6]

Summary

Consumers are more frequently punishing companies that do not trade or advertise ethically. Ethics therefore need to be high on the agenda of every advertising professional and every advertising agency. Consumers are also prepared to pay more for ethical brands. Honest advertising makes a company seem more ethical in the eyes of consumers.

However, ethical advertising can still go hand-in-hand with commercial imperatives. Doing business to satisfy a societal need – a shared value – not only helps companies to grow, but also allows them to regain their credibility in the eyes of society.

Practical inspiration

1 Is your sector or your brand under social pressure and, if so, how do you deal with it? Reactively or proactively? Is the pressure increasing or decreasing?

2 Does your company have a specific ethical standard for advertising and how do you translate this standard into practice in your dealings with advertising agencies?

3 Are you convinced that today's consumers are willing to pay more for ethical brands?

4 Is CSR a central pillar of your company strategy and are its objectives quantified? Are you implementing a CSR plan? How is progress in this area communicated?

5 Apply the concept of share value to your brand strategy.

CASE STUDY   IBM: 'Smarter Planet Outcomes'

In 2008, IBM wanted to show that it's about more than just information and services. By launching its 'Smarter Planet' strategy, the brand established a higher purpose and showed its contribution to society. Since then, IBM has been working continuously with its customers, governments and other partners to realize its vision. As part of its supporting marketing campaign, in 2011, IBM wanted to show people what a smarter planet can really mean, using a series of concrete examples. Via an integrated campaign, the results of a number of breakthrough applications were communicated to the general public. This resulted in a 25 per cent boost for the IBM share price and second place in the 2011 'Best Global Brands Survey' by Interbrand. In the meantime, two-thirds of the company's target group now has a positive attitude towards IBM. A perfect example of how profit and ethics can work together, of how stakeholder value equals shareholder value, and thus well worth the award of a bronze Euro Effie in 2012.

SOURCE Warc (2012). IBM: Let's Build A Smarter Planet. Consulted online: www.warc.com

Notes

1   Public Interest Research Centre and WWF UK [accessed 3 March 2012] Think Of Me As Evil? Opening the ethical debate in advertising, *Common Cause* [Online] http://assets.wwf.org.uk/downloads/think_of_me_as_evil.pdf

2   Upstream and YouGov [accessed 18 March 2012] Digital Advertising Attitudes Report, *Upstream* [Online] http://upstreamsystems.com/2012-digital-advertising-attitude-report-the-consequences-of-digital-ad-bombardment

3   Beltramini, R F (2011) From platitudes to principles: an advertising ethics call to action, *Journal of Advertising Research*, September, pp 475–76

4   Snyder, W (2011) Making the case for enhanced advertising ethics: how a new way of thinking about advertising ethics may build consumer trust, *Journal of Advertising Research*, 51 (3), pp 477–83

5   Porter, M E and Kramer, M R (2011) Creating shared value, *Harvard Business Review*, Jan–Feb 2011, pp 62–77

6   Polman, P (2012) Captain Planet, *Harvard Business Review*, June 2012, pp 112–18

✧ **Conclusion** ✧
Advertising is dead – long live advertising

Today, advertising has reached yet another turning point. But this is by no means the first time in its history. In order to survive, 20th-century advertising media will have to evolve to become true and platform-independent cross media brands.

In a way, they will need to become hybrid media as well, realizing different communication functions and goals. New media will have to demonstrate their effectiveness and sustainability both in the short and in the long term. They will have to prove they are more than just hype. While evolving, these media will increasingly face the boundaries posed by a rising concern about privacy amongst consumer groups and governments.

Future advertising strategies will depend on the power of collaboration with consumers and interaction with the world. This leads us to five important conclusions:

Learn to survive with the new consumer

A large part of a brand's customer base is made up of irregular buyers, the so-called 'light buyers'. It is a group that continues to become increasingly important: one out of every two brand customers in different categories is a light buyer. More than ever, consumers have relationships with different brands. With its reach and measurable effectiveness, advertising is very successful with this group of light buyers. In order to make a brand grow over time, a penetration strategy aimed at the acquisition of light buyers is more effective than a frequency strategy.

In a volatile environment, brands know less and less who their future customers will be. High brand awareness is a basic condition for hitting the mental shortlist of these consumers. This brand awareness and preference is built and maintained by advertising: in the minds of the consumer, these brands guarantee a good price/quality ratio, inspire confidence, make brands reliable and exude quality – or so the research indicates.[1]

Some pundits claim that 'cool' brands invest little or nothing in advertising. But the contrary appears to be true. A brand like Apple – the company with the largest market capitalization in the world in 2012 – invested about $1.1 billion in advertising in 2012 (56.8 per cent more than in 2011). For the launch of the iPad alone, Apple spent around $457 million in 2010, which is roughly what Barack Obama spent on his 2012 election campaign.[2]

Advertising has a double effect: there is the direct effect on the consumer, but also the indirect – even more powerful – effect via so-called opinion-leaders and influencers. These opinion-makers mostly get their stories and inspiration from mass media. Approximately one in every three consumer conversations about brands is directly inspired by advertising, according to recent Belgian research. In most cases, consumer conversations about brands are positive. Established brands are talked about the most.[3]

Build an advertising ecosystem

The marketing campaigns discussed in this book are without exception skilful applications of an integrated marketing communications strategy. Based on a focused strategy and a creative concept, they all use different means of communication that complement and strengthen each other, in order to obtain the desired results. And in every case, the brands concerned saw their market share and sales rise in the short or medium to long term. In all these award-winning campaigns, advertising through mass media played a pivotal role in the successful execution of the campaign strategy, in some cases supported by activation programmes and the so-called 'new media' channels. The media mix of the future will, above all, be complementary. In this respect, the traditional AIDA effect model and the new ADIA model seem to merge seamlessly: from customer acquisition to customer relationship-building.

Interaction and cross-fertilization between the different available media are becoming more and more important. More specifically, social media can give a dynamic and lively dimension to advertising, thanks to their interactive and participative qualities. There is said to be a real leverage effect towards consumers. Sociologist Manuel Castells talks of 'mass self-communication', generated by individual consumers and potentially reaching a very large audience.[4] Nevertheless, the 1/10/90 rule remains valid here: 90 per cent of social media users are just passive spectators. Likewise, 9 out of every 10 conversations about brands still occur face to face, while only 1 in 10 occur via so-called social media.[5]

Consumers are strongly influenced by their social environment, via mass media and opinion makers (whether offline or online). The public image of brands – as shaped by advertising – is what largely determines the individual brand image held by consumers.[6] This is particularly true for brands with an important self-expressive value.

In the light of this evolution, it is more appropriate to consider the idea of a true advertising ecosystem, rather than talking about integrated marketing communication. Integrating marketing communication goals and means is a necessary, yet rather mechanical, process. An ecosystem is organic and more fluid. Instead of focusing on the role of the consumer, it takes the living environment of the total human being as its starting point.

Know your place in the world of the 'cons-human'

In my book *Het Merk Mens*, published in 2007, I pointed out that the difference between consumers and citizens is slowly disappearing. Everybody is now both a customer and a citizen, a consumer and a human being. In fact, a 'cons-human'. People want to satisfy their needs as a consumer, but embedded in a socially responsible context. Consumer experience and citizenship increasingly coexist. This does not stop people from having to deal with the conflicting demands of these dual roles from time to time. Finding and keeping the right balance is not always easy.[7]

In general, people are still driven more often by their roles as consumers than by their roles as socially involved citizens. It is no surprise that the economic crisis has amplified price sensitivity among consumers, and user-friendliness and/or product and service quality continue to outweigh arguments about serving the common good. In their role as consumers, people are likely to make choices based on their own personal needs and priorities.

These choices often have little to do with the values they uphold as citizens. When considering something of such a transactional nature as purchasing, sustainability arguments are often beaten into second place by commercial arguments.[8]

Sustainability arguments do, however, become more important when the consumer and citizen roles are not competing. Sustainable solutions that appeal to us as consumers and citizens alike are therefore more likely to gain support. Think about cars that are fuel-efficient, while offering a unique driving experience at the same time. Or, even more preferable, about fiscal support for environmentally friendly projects, as is the case with the installation of solar panels in Europe.

In their decision-making process, consumers are looking for the right balance between self-interest and public interest. Brands and their advertising can help consumers to find this balance. In this sense, consumers are indeed also stakeholders.

When it comes to brands, the 'cons-human' is more than ever in the driver's seat. Consumers that 'like' or 'share' mainly do this to express or highlight their own personality. They only support these brands implicitly. Consumers 'use' brands and their advertising in the context of social media, in order to create their own brand profile. Brands that are self-expressive by nature therefore have a significantly higher chance of being 'liked' or 'shared'.

Brands need to be well aware of their role in this new world in which the 'cons-human' is calling the shots. Brands wanting to play a prominent part in this age of consumer performance need to enhance their aspirational and self-expressive nature in order to score.[9]

Make the difference with an ISP (Integrated Selling Proposition)

Brands with a strong image prefer to focus on the relevance and instrumental advantages of innovations and brand extensions. In this way, they present themselves as forward-looking and vital, by aiming to make the lives of consumers better and more pleasant.

New brands need to build a brand personality and therefore tend to focus on consumer emotions. Only when a brand has acquired a unique personality in the mind of the consumer will this brand appear on the mental shortlist.

Strong brand personality is an absolute condition for entering into a sustainable relationship with consumers. Advertising has proven its ability to add a strong personality to products. This personality is the basis for consumers to enter into a long-term relationship with brands.[10] Brands without a personality downgrade themselves to generic products, limited to mere instrumental transactions with consumers, based on the lowest price.

Brands are increasingly aiming to promote higher social ideals in their campaigns as well. They want to 'improve' the lives of consumers. They adhere to a set of higher ethical standards and encourage their customers to behave socially and responsibly. By doing so, brands are building a conscience. An analysis of leading global brands shows that they combine USPs and ESPs in their communication, almost without exception. They communicate about relevance, while simultaneously building their brand personality.

In many instances they opt for social communication. Moreover, they use these channels for more than their corporate communication alone. By following a strategy of higher ideals, a corresponding social commitment is reflected in the product that is marketed. In this way, social and economic added value is created. This strategy has not done the brands concerned any financial harm at all. In fact, they have proven to be 400 times more profitable than the average on the Standard & Poor's (S&P) 500 (the listing America's 500 leading companies by market capitalization).[11]

There was a time when USPs, ESPs and 'noble purposes' were considered to be contradictory advertising strategies; strategies asking for choices to be made. Today, strong brands work concurrently with this strategic 'trinity'. In some cases they do this in different campaigns working at different levels (product/corporate), but in an increasing number of cases the 'trinity' is integrated into a single campaign. This is the era of the integrated selling proposition (ISP).

The ISP allows the consumer to feel a stronger sense of identification and empathy, both for him- and herself and towards others. Advertising helps to build a personality, a character, a culture for products. It is this unique personality, based on direct and indirect brand exposures and experiences, that enables consumers to enter into a relationship with the brand.[12]

FIGURE 12.1   How the ISP (integrated selling proposition) works

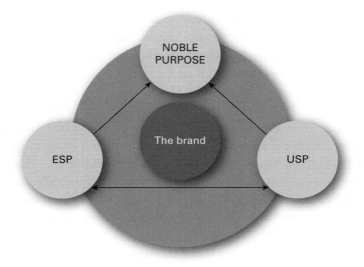

A strong brand communicates using informative and emotional messages (USP and ESP), but also appeals to higher ideals in order to convince consumers. A balanced mix of messages leads to better results and profitability.

(Source: Think BBDO)

Time for advertising that sticks

It almost seems like a paradox: in times when consumers are complaining more and more that they are irritated by advertising, advertising movies (some lasting several minutes) are now being shared by millions of consumers all over the world via social media. How can this be explained? The answer is simple: these people are watching advertising that sticks.

People get more annoyed by bad advertising than by the total quantity of advertising as a whole. Research shows that campaign owe three-quarters of their success to the content and style of the advertising itself. 'Creativity is king.' Yet in all fairness, creative advertising will not succeed in selling a bad product.[13]

In addition, creative advertising stimulates brand recall, an important condition for standing out in the consumer's (especially the light buyer's) mental shortlist. Moreover, creative advertising is not commitment-free, since it only works when it is both original and relevant. In this respect, advertising (and media planning) needs to integrate seamlessly into the consumer's context. It must take account of the consumer's stage of life and/or the different roles he or she can assume at the same time (for example, a woman as a mother, partner, colleague or friend). The same person with the same personality can behave and act differently, depending on the social context in which they find themselves. Advertising – and advertising planning – must always consider the social environment of the individual consumer.[14]

It is advertising that sticks which makes a brand rise above the crowd. Brands that want to (re)confirm their position as market leaders barely differentiate from each other. It is advertising that can make the difference, by being divergent, by drawing attention, by lodging in the memory, by being talked about and shared by consumers. It is advertising that results in word of mouth amongst consumers, both directly and indirectly (via the so-called opinion-makers). It is advertising that entertains consumers and breaks through the barrier of irritation. It is advertising that is shared by millions around the world. It is advertising that connects people. The future of advertising is called 'creativity that sticks'.

So what is our final conclusion? Is advertising dead or alive? Twentieth-century advertising is certainly dead. Twenty-first-century advertising will have to reinvent itself in order to survive. This transformation is going on as we speak. What is more, brands that invest in advertising during an economic recession have been shown to surmount that recession faster and stronger. Times of crisis are typically moments when the consumer's mental pecking order is being shaken up, when brand market shares are shifting. Advertising can be a determining factor for the future of brands.

Hopefully, this book has provided new insights and strong foundations that will enable marketers and managers to better face this new reality. Consequently, it is not only a guide but also a source of reflection and inspiration for the strategic questions that are emerging in today's practice.

Please do not forget to send me your questions, thoughts or suggestions via **www.advertisingtransformed.com** In this way, you'll be helping to write a new chapter for it.

Notes

1　Kapferer, J N (2008) *The New Strategic Brand Management*, Kogan Page, London

2　Delo, C (2012) Despite record spending, political advertising has yet to hit ceiling, *Advertising Age*, **83** (41), p 10

3　Zemni, H (2012) All media are social! Yes they are, InSitesConsulting Report

4　Castells, M (2009) *Communication Power*, Oxford University Press, New York

5　Keller, E and Fay, B (2012) *The Face-to-Face Book: Why real relationships rule in a digital marketplace*, Free Press, New York

6　Franzen, G and Moriarty, S (2009) *The Science and Art of Branding*, ME Sharpe, New York

7　Van Dyck, F (2007) *Het Merk Mens*, LannooCampus/Scriptum, Tielt

8　Walker Smith, J (2012) 10 trends in sustainability, *Admap*, September 2012, pp 14–15

9　Wallace, E, Buil, I and de Chernatony, L (2012) Facebook 'friendship' and brand advocacy, *Journal of Brand Management*, **20** (2), pp 128–46

10　Keller, K L (2008) *Strategic Brand Management*, Pearson International Edition

11　Stengel, J (2011) *Grow*, Crown Business, New York

12　Franzen, G, op cit, p 233

13　Hallward, J (2007) *Gimme! The human nature of successful marketing*, John Wiley & Sons, New Jersey

14　Franzen, G, op cit, p 232

INDEX

NB: page numbers in *italic* indicate figures or tables